# Life of Mrs. Mary Jemison: Deh-He-Wä-Mis

RELATING HER HISTORY TO THE AUTHOR

# Life of Mrs. Mary Jemison: Deh-He-Wä-Mis

The Ordeals and Life of a Young Settler Girl
Captured by Indians
During the French and Indian War

James E. Seaver

LEONAUR

*Life of Mrs. Mary Jemison:*
*Deh-He-Wä-Mis*
*The Ordeals and Life of a Young Settler Girl Captured by Indians*
*During the French and Indian War*
by James E. Seaver

First published under the title
*Life of Mrs. Mary Jemison,*
*Deh-He-Wä-Mis*

Leonaur is an imprint of Oakpast Ltd

Copyright in this form © 2011 Oakpast Ltd

ISBN: 978-0-85706-779-1 (hardcover)
ISBN: 978-0-85706-780-7 (softcover)

http://www.leonaur.com

Publisher's Notes

# Contents

# Original Publisher's Note

The life of Mary Jemison was one of singular vicissitude and trial. Taken captive at the early age of thirteen years, and trained in the wilderness to the ordinary duties of the Indian female, she became imbued with their sentiments, and transformed essentially into one of their number. Born on the sea, as it were the child of accident, made an orphan by the tomahawk of the red man, it was her sad destiny to become lost to the race from which she sprung, and affiliated with the one which she had every reason to abhor. This transformation, the reverse of the order of nature, was perfected by her becoming the wife of an Indian, and the mother of Indian children. As if in punishment of this unnatural alliance, two of her sons with a violent death at the hands of their brother. and afterward, to complete the tragedy, the fratricide himself dies by the hand of violence.

Notwithstanding the severity of these domestic calamities and the toilsome life she was forced to lead, she met her trials with fortitude, and lived to the great age of ninety-one years. Her life, however, was not without its "sunny side." She found attached friends among her Seneca kindred, and was ever treated by them with consideration and kindness. The esteem and affection with which she was cherished is indicated by the liberal provision made for her by the Seneca chiefs, before they disposed of their hereditary domain. They ceded to her in fee-simple, and for her individual use, the "Gardeau Reservation" upon the Genesee River, which contained upward of nineteen thousand acres of land; and thus raised her and her posterity to an affluence beyond the utmost dreams of the imagination, had she chosen afterward to retain it, and return to civilized life. It was not the least hardship of her case, that, when liberty and restoration were finally offered, and urged upon her, she found they came too late for her acceptance; and she was forced to fulfil her destiny by dying, as she had lived, a Seneca woman.

The narrative of her life cannot fail to awaken our sympathies, while it may serve to remind us of the perils which surrounded our fathers during the period of colonization. As time wears away we are apt to forget, in the fullness of our present security, the dangers which surrounded the founders of the original colonies, from the period of the French and Indian war to the close of the Revolution. It is well not to lose our familiarity with these trying scenes, lest we become insensible of our ever-continuing debt of gratitude to those who met those dangers manfully, to secure to their descendants the blessings we now enjoy. This narrative, while it brings to light a few of the darkest transactions of our early history, is not without some instruction.

It is proper to state that this work was first published in 1824, during the lifetime of Mrs. Jemison, and that shortly afterward, the author, to whose diligence we are indebted for the preservation of the incidents of her history. himself deceased. In 1842, the work was revised by Ebenezer Mix, Esq., who also added chapters 5, 8, and 15, and the four articles in the Appendix.

The frequent inquiries made for the work of the publisher since it went out of print induced him to undertake the publication of the present edition. The engraving which forms the frontispiece and also the illustrations are new, and were designed for this edition. As the progress of Indian research, made since that day, has revealed some errors in the text, numerous footnotes, historical and geographical, have been added, corrective or explanatory, which are now, for the first time. published with the original narrative.

Rochester, N.Y., March,

8

# Introduction

The peace which was concluded between the United States and Great Britain in 1783 led to a treaty of peace and amnesty between the United States and the Indian confederacy called the Six Nations, which took place at Fort Stanwix, (now Rome, N.Y.,) in 1784, conducted by commissioners on the part of the United States, and the chiefs, warriors, and head men of the Six Nations, on their part.

By this treaty, all the prisoners who had been taken and were at that time retained by the Indians were to be set at liberty. On this joyful event, those prisoners who had escaped the tomahawk, the gauntlet, and the sacrificial fire, were released from bondage, and restored to their friends, to society, and to the world. Although the number of prisoners thus released were few, in proportion to the great number who had been taken, they were so numerous that their return brought the legends of torture and death to every section of the country. These horrid tales required not the aid of fiction, or the persuasive powers of rhetoric, to heighten their colourings, or gain credence to their shocking truths. In those days, Indian barbarities were the constant topic of the domestic fireside, the parlour, the hall, and the forum. It is presumed that, at this time, there are but few native citizens that have passed the middle age who do not distinctly recollect of hearing such frightful accounts of Indian barbarities, oft repeated, in the nursery and in the family circle, until it almost caused their hair to stand erect, and deprived them of the power of motion.

Time, however, has produced a confusion of incidents in those tales, and enveloped the fidelity of their transmission to us in clouds of doubt. To rescue from oblivion, and preserve in their primitive purity, some of those legends, and to exemplify and record, for the use of posterity as well as for the present generation, a faithful delineation of the characteristic traits of the Iroquois, is the object of these memoirs.

At the same treaty, the Six Nations, or Iroquois, were left in undisturbed possession of the greater portion of the state of New York, and had the right of possession guaranteed to them by the United States of all the territory west of a line called the property line, running nearly parallel with, and less than eighty miles west of the Hudson River, two small tracts excepted. At this time, Mary Jemison had been with the Indians twenty-nine years—seven had transpired during the French war with the British, in which the Six Nations raised the tomahawk against the British and Americans; and seven during the revolutionary war, in which the Indians arrayed themselves on the side of the British against the Americans; there being an interval of peace of fifteen years between—if peace it could be called—when they were constantly sending war parties against other Indian tribes, south and north, from the torrid to the frigid zone, and west to the Rocky Mountains.

During this time, Mrs. Jemison had been twice married to Indian chiefs, and had a husband and seven children then living. She, too, was nearly two hundred miles from any white settlement, and knew not that she had a white relative or friend on earth: she, therefore, resolved not to accept of her freedom, but to spend the remainder of her days with the Indians, where she knew she had affectionate relatives and many kind friends. This resolution she carried fully into effect, and became their faithful and correct chronicler for more than three-fourths of a century.

At this time., 1784, and for years afterward, no settlements of white people were made in the state west of Cherry Valley, on the headwaters of the Susquehanna, and the German Flats, on the Mohawk, as those places were situated nearly as far west as the property line, the boundary of the Indian lands. So fresh were the wounds which the whites had received from their savage neighbours, that the Indians were viewed with a jealous eye, even when unmolested and unprovoked. Under these circumstances, peaceable citizens were little inclined to trespass on their lands, or give them the least pretext for a quarrel, by even travelling into their country. No white people, therefore, visited their villages, except some half-savage traders, and a few of the refuse of society, who, to escape the meshes of civil or criminal law, bade *adieu* to civilized life, and took shelter in the recesses of the forest, under the protection of its lords.

The Indian title to the lands surrounding Mrs. Jemison's residence was not sold to the whites until the great Council in 1797, when may be dated the first time of her associating with moral, social, civilized man, from the time of her childhood, after the lapse of forty-two years. Still, she had retained her native language with great purity; and had treasured up, and constantly kept in her own breast, all those moral and social virtues, by the precepts of which civilized society professes to be guided, and by their directions always to be governed.

At length, the richness and fertility of the soil excited emigration; and here and there a family settled down and commenced improvements in the country which had recently been the property of the aborigines. Those who settled near the Genesee River soon became acquainted with "The White Woman," as Mrs. Jemison was called, whose history they anxiously sought, both as a matter of interest and curiosity. Frankness characterized her conduct, and without reserve she would readily gratify them by relating some of the most important periods of her life.

Although her bosom companions, as an ancient warrior, and not-withstanding her children and associates were all Indians, yet it was found that she possessed an uncommon share of hospitality, and that her friendship was well worth courting and preserving. Her house was the stranger's home: from her table the hungry were refreshed; she made the naked as comfortable as her means would admit; and in all her actions, discovered so much natural goodness of heart, that her admirers increased in proportion to the extension of her acquaintance, and she became celebrated as the friend of the distressed. She was the protectress of the homeless fugitive, and made welcome the weary wanderer. Many still live, (as at time of first publication), to commemorate her benevolence toward them when prisoners during the war, and to ascribe their deliverance to the mediation of "The White Woman."

The settlements of civilized society increased around her, and the whole country was inhabited by a rich and respectable people, principally from New England, as much distinguished for their spirit of inquisitiveness as for their habits of industry and honesty, who had all heard from one source and another a part of her life in detached pieces, and had obtained an idea that the whole taken in connection would afford instruction and amusement.

Many gentlemen of respectability felt anxious that her narrative might be laid before the public, with a view not only to perpetuate the remembrance of the atrocities of the savages in former times, but to preserve some historical facts which they supposed to be intimately connected with her life, and which otherwise must be lost.

Forty years had passed since the close of the Revolutionary war, and almost seventy years had seen Mrs. Jemison with the Indians, when Daniel W. Banister, Esq., at the instance of several gentlemen, and prompted by his own ambition to add something to the accumulating fund of useful knowledge, resolved, in the autumn of 1823, to embrace that time, while she was capable of recollecting and reciting the scenes through which she had passed, to collect from herself, and to publish to the world, an accurate account of her life.

I was employed to collect the materials, and prepare the work for the press; and accordingly went to the house of Mrs. Jennet Whaley, in the town of Castile, Genesee County, N.Y., in company with the publisher, who procured the interesting subject of the following narrative to come to that place, (a distance of four miles,) and there repeat the story of her eventful life. She came on foot, in company with Mr. Thomas Clute, whom she considered her protector, and tarried several days; which time was busily occupied in taking a sketch of her narrative as she recited it.

In stature, she is very short, considerably under the middle size; but stands tolerably erect, with her head bent forward, apparently from her having for a long time been accustomed to carrying heavy burdens, supported by a strap placed across her forehead. Her complexion is very white for a woman of her age, and although the wrinkles of fourscore years are deeply indented in her cheeks, yet the crimson of youth is distinctly visible. Her eyes are light blue, a little faded by age, but naturally brilliant and sparkling. Her sight is quite dim, though she is able to perform her necessary labour without the assistance of glasses. Her cheek-bones are high, and rather prominent: and her front teeth, in the lower jaw. are sound and good. When she looks up, and is engaged in conversation, her countenance is very expressive; but from her long residence with the Indians, she has acquired the habit of peeping from under the eyebrows, as they do, with the head inclined downward. Formerly, her hair was of a light chestnut brown; it is now quite gray, a little curled, of middling length, and tied in a bunch behind. She informed me that she had never worn a cap or a comb.

She speaks English plainly and distinctly, slightly tinged with the Irish idiom, and has the use of words so well as to render herself intelligible on any subject with which she is acquainted. Her recollection and memory exceeded my expectation. It cannot be reasonably supposed that a person of her age has kept the events of seventy years in so complete a chain as to be able to assign to each its proper time and place. She, however, made her recital with as few obvious mistakes as might be expected from a person of fifty. Indeed, in every case, where she attempted to give dates, she was remarkably correct,—so uniformly so that she coincided exactly with history, except in one instance, which was the surrender of Fort Du Quesne by the French to the English; and this is more to be attributed to her ignorance at the time than to the treachery of her memory, for the fort was always filled with English or Yankee traders, trappers, hunters, and outlaws, as well as Frenchmen; and the Ohio Indians knew little and cared less who commanded the fort, so long as they could trade there to suit themselves. Under such circumstances, it is not remarkable that a young woman, fifteen or sixteen years old, domesticated among the Indians, and residing three or four hundred miles from the fort, should not know the precise time that the French flag was struck and the English hoisted in its stead; which absolutely took place in 1758, while she resided in that country.

She walks with a quick step, without a staff, and can yet cross a stream on a log or pole as steadily as any other person. Her passions are easily excited. At a number of periods in her narration, tears trickled down her grief-worn cheek, and at the same time a rising sigh would stop her utterance.

Industry is a virtue which she has uniformly practiced from the day of her adoption to the present. She pounds her *samp*, cooks for herself, gathers and chops her wood, feeds her cattle and poultry, and performs other laborious services. Last season, she planted, tended, and gathered her corn; in short, she is always busy.

Her dress, at the time I saw her, was made and worn after the usual Indian fashion. She had on a brown, undressed flannel short-gown, with long sleeves, the skirt reaching to the hips, being tied before in two places with deer-skin strings; below the skirt of the gown was to be seen three or four inches of the lower extremity of a cotton shirt, which was without collar or sleeves, and open before. Her petticoat, or the Indian substitute for that garment, was composed of about a yard and a quarter of blue broadcloth, with the lists on, and sewed together at the ends. This was tied around her waist, or rather above her hips, under her shirt, with a string, in such a manner as to leave one-fourth of a yard or more of the top of the cloth to be turned over the string, and display the top list, and four or five inches of the cloth below the bottom of the shirt—the main body of the garment and the other list reaching down to the calves of her legs; below which was to be seen her leggins, consisting of pieces of blue broadcloth, wrapped around her legs, and tied or pinned on, reaching from her knees to just within the tops of her buckskin *moccasins*. She wore no footings or socks on her feet at any season, unless some rags wrapped around her toes could be considered such. Over her shoulders was wrapped a common Indian or Dutch blanket, and on her head she wore an old, brown woollen cloth, somewhat in the shape of a sun-bonnet.

Thus attired—and it will be recollected that she was not caught in her *dishabille*, as she had come from home, the distance of four miles, for the express purpose of meeting us—thus attired, I say, we met the owner of two square miles of very fertile and productive land, lying in the midst of a dense population, and near an excellent market—with an annuity of three hundred dollars a year, secured to her, her heirs, and assigns forever. Yet such was the dress this woman was not only contented to wear but delighted in wearing. Habit having rendered it convenient and comfortable, she wore it as a matter of choice.

Her house, in which she lives, is twenty by twenty eight feet; built of square timber, with a shingled roof and a framed stoop. In the centre of the house is a chimney of stones and sticks, in which there are two fireplaces. She has a good framed barn, twenty-six by thirty-six, well filled, and owns a line stock of cattle and horses. Besides the buildings above mentioned, she owns a number of buildings occupied by tenants, who work her flats upon shares.

Her dwelling is on the west side of Genesee River, about one hundred rods north of the Great Slide—a curiosity which will hereafter be described.

Mrs. Jemison appeared sensible of her ignorance of the manners of the white people, and for that reason was not familiar, except with those with whom she was intimately acquainted. In fact, she was, to, appearance, so jealous of her rights, or afraid that she should thing that would be injurious to herself or family, that if Mr. Clute had not been present, we should have been unable to have obtained her history. She, however, soon became free and unembarrassed in her conversation, and spoke with a degree of mildness, candour, and simplicity, that is calculated to remove all doubts as to the veracity of the speaker. The vices of the Indians she appeared to palliate, or at least not to aggravate, and seemed to take pride in extolling their virtues. A kind of family pride inclined her to withhold whatever would blot the character of her descendants, and perhaps induced her to keep back many things that would have been interesting.

For the life of her last husband we are indebted to her cousin, Mr. George Jemison, to whom she referred us for information on that subject generally. The thoughts of his deeds, probably, chilled her old heart, and made her dread to rehearse them; and at the same time she well knew they were no secret, for she had frequently heard him relate the whole, not only to her cousin but to others.

Before she left us, she was very sociable, and she resumed her naturally pleasant countenance, enlivened with a smile.

Her neighbors speak of her as possessing one of the happiest tempers and dispositions, and give her the name of never having done a censurable act to their knowledge.

Her habits are those of the Indians—she sleeps on skins without a bedstead; sits upon the floor, or on a bench; and when she eats, holds her victuals on her lap, or in her hands.

Her ideas of religion correspond in every respect with those of the great mass of the Senecas. She applauds virtue, and condemns vice. She believes in a future state, in which the good will be happy, and the bad miserable; and that the acquisition of that happiness depends primarily upon human volition, and the consequent good of the happy recipient of blessedness. But she is a stranger to the doctrines of the Christian religion.

Her daughters are said to be active and enterprising women; and her grandsons, who have arrived to manhood, are considered able, decent, and respectable men, in their tribe, and many of them are greeted with respect in civilized society.

Having in a cursory manner introduced the principal subject of the following pages, I proceed to the narration of a life that has been viewed with attention, for a great number of years, by a few, and which will be read by the public with mixed sensations of pleasure and pain, joy and sorrow, and with interest, anxiety, and satisfaction.

Pembroke, March

# Letter From Ely S. Parker,

Do-Ne-Ho-Ga-Weh, a Seneca *Sachem.*

<br>

Norfolk, Mch. 24th, 1856.

D. M. Dewey, Esq.,

Dear Sir:

Yours of the 12th is received, and I am very happy to know that you are republishing the *Life of Mary Jemison*, the "White Woman."

Many years ago, I perused Seaver's book with great interest, and have since had good opportunity of testing its reliability, by comparing it with the traditional history preserved of her among the Indians with whom she lived and died, all of which more than corroborates every incident related in the narrative. I have, therefore, every reason to believe it to be entirely true. *I* am, with respect,

Yours truly,

E. S. Parker,

Do-Ne-Ho-Ga-Weh.

# CHAPTER 1

# Parentage of Mary Jemison

Although I may have frequently heard the history of my ancestry, my recollection is too imperfect to enable me to trace it further back than to my father and mother, whom I have often heard mention the families from whence they originated, as having possessed wealth, and honourable stations under the government of the country in which they resided.

On account of the great length of time that has elapsed since I was separated from my parents and friends, and having heard the story of their nativity only in the days of my childhood, I am unable to state positively which of the two countries, Ireland or Scotland, was the land of my parents' birth and education. It, however, is my impression, that they were born and brought up in Ireland.

My father's name was Thomas Jemison, and my mother's, before her marriage, was Jane Erwin. Their affection for each other was mutual, and of that happy kind which tends directly to sweeten the cup of life; to render connubial sorrows lighter; to assuage every discontentment; and to promote not only their own comfort, but that of all who come within the circle of their acquaintance. Of their happiness, I recollect to have heard them often speak; and the remembrance I yet retain of their mildness and perfect agreement in the government of their children, together with their mutual attention to our common education, manners, religious instruction and wants, renders it certain in my mind that they were ornaments to the married state, and examples of connubial love worthy of imitation. After my remembrance, they were strict observers of religious duties; for it was the daily practice of my father, morning and evening, to attend, in his family, to the worship of God.

Resolved to leave the land of their nativity, they removed from their residence to a port in Ireland, where they lived but a short time before they set sail for this country, in the year 1742 or 1743, on board the ship *William and Mary*, bound to Philadelphia.

The intestine divisions, civil wars, and ecclesiastical rigidity and domination that prevailed in those days, were the causes of their leaving their mother country, to find a home in the American wilderness, under the mild and temperate government of the descendants of William Penn; where they might worship God according to the dictates of their own consciences, and pursue their lawful avocations without fear of molestation.

In Europe, my parents had two sons and one daughter; their names were John, Thomas, and Betsey; with whom, after having put their effects on board, they embarked, leaving a large connection of relatives and friends, under all those painful sensations which are only felt when kindred souls give the parting hand and last farewell to those to whom they are endeared by every friendly tie.

During their voyage I was born—to be the sport of fortune and almost an outcast to civil society; to stem the current of adversity through a long chain of vicissitudes, unsupported by the advice of tender parents, or the hand of an affectionate friend; and even without the enjoyment, from others, of any of those tender sympathies which are calculated to sweeten the joys of life, except such as naturally flow from uncultivated minds, that have been rendered callous by ferocity.

Excepting my birth, nothing remarkable occurred to my parents on their passage; and they were safely landed at Philadelphia. My father being fond of rural life, and having been bred to agricultural pursuits, soon left the city, and removed his family to a tract of excellent land lying on Marsh Creek, on the frontier settlement of Pennsylvania. At that place, he cleared a large farm; and for seven or eight years enjoyed the fruits of his industry. Peace attended their labours; and they had nothing to alarm them, save the midnight howl of the prowling wolf, or the terrifying shriek of the ferocious panther, as they occasionally visited the improvements to take a lamb or a calf to satisfy their hunger.

During this period my mother had two sons, between whose ages there was a difference of about three years. The oldest was named Matthew, and the other Robert.

Health presided on every countenance, and vigour and strength characterized every exertion. Our mansion was a little paradise. The morning of my childish, happy days, will ever stand fresh in my memory, notwithstanding the many severe trials through which I have passed, in arriving at my present situation, at so advanced an age. Even at this remote period, the recollection of my pleasant home at my father's, of my parents, of my brothers and sister, and of the manner in which I was deprived of them all at once, affects me so powerfully that I am almost overwhelmed with grief that is seemingly insupportable. Frequently, I dream of those happy days: but alas! they are gone; they have left me to be carried through a long life, dependent for the little pleasures of nearly seventy years upon the tender mercies of the Indians! In the spring of 1752, and through the succeeding seasons, the stories of Indian barbarities inflicted upon the whites in those days frequently excited in my parents the most serious alarm for our safety.

The next year, the storm gathered faster; many murders were committed; and many captives were exposed to meet death in its most frightful form, by having their bodies stuck full of pine splinters, which were immediately set on fire, while their tormentors were exulting in their distress and rejoicing in their agony.

In 1754, an army for the protection of the settlers, and to drive back the French and Indians, was raised from the militia of the colonial governments, and placed, secondarily, under the command of Colonel George Washington. In that army I had an uncle, whose name was John Jemison, who was killed at the battle of the Great Meadows, or Fort Necessity. His wife, had died some time before this, and left a young child, which my mother nursed in the most tender manner, till its mother's sister took it away, a few months after my uncle's death. The French and Indians, after the surrender of Fort Necessity by Colonel Washington, (which happened the same season, and soon after his victory over them at that place.) grew more and more terrible. The death of the whites, and the plundering and burning of their property, was apparently their only object. But as yet we had not heard the death-yell, nor seen the smoke of a dwelling that had been lit by an Indian's hand.

The return of a New-Year's day found us unmolested; and though we knew that the enemy was at no great distance from us, my father concluded that he would continue to occupy his land another season, expecting, probably from the great exertions which the government was then making, that as soon as the troops could commence their operations in the spring, the enemy would be conquered, and compelled to agree to a treaty of peace.

In the preceding autumn, my father either moved to another part of his farm, or to another neighbourhood, a short distance from our former abode. I well recollect moving, and that the barn that was on the place we moved to was built of logs, though the house was a good one.

The winter of 1754–5, was as mild as common fall seasons; and spring presented a pleasant seedtime, and indicated a plenteous harvest. My father, with the assistance of his oldest sons, repaired his farm as usual, and was daily preparing the soil for the reception of seed. His cattle and sheep were numerous, and according to the best idea of wealth that I can now form, he was wealthy.

But alas! how transitory are all human affairs! how fleeting are riches! how brittle the invisible thread on which all earthly comforts are suspended! Peace in a moment can take an immeasurable flight; health lose its rosy checks; and life will vanish like a vapour at the appearance of the sun! In one fatal day, our prospects were all blasted; and death, by cruel hands, inflicted upon almost the whole of the family.

My education had received as much attention from my parents as their situation in a new country would admit. I had been at school some, where I learned to read in a book that was about half as large as a Bible; and in the Bible I had read a little. I had also learned the Catechism, which I used frequently to repeat to my parents; and every night, before I went to bed, I was obliged to stand up before my mother, and repeat some words that I suppose was a prayer.

My reading, catechism, and prayers, I have long since forgotten; though, for a number of the first years that I lived with the Indians, I repeated the prayers as often as I had an opportunity. After the revolutionary war, I remembered the names of some of the letters when I saw them; but have never read a word since I was taken prisoner. It is but a few years since a missionary kindly gave me a Bible, which I am very fond of hearing my neighbours read to me, and should be pleased to learn to read it myself; but my sight for a number of years has been so dim that I have not been able to distinguish one letter from another.

## Chapter 2

# Whole Family Taken Captive in 1755

On a pleasant day in the spring of 1755, when my father was sowing flax-seed, and my brothers driving the teams, I was sent to a neighbour's house, a distance of perhaps a mile, to procure a horse, and return with it the next morning. I went as I was directed. I went out of the house to which I had been sent in the beginning of the evening, and saw a sheet, wide spread, approaching toward me, in which I was caught, as I have ever since believed, and deprived of my senses. The family soon found me on the ground, almost lifeless, as they said; took me in, and made use of every remedy in their power for my recovery; but without effect, till daybreak, when my senses returned, and I soon found myself in good health, so that I went home with the horse very early in the morning.

The appearance of that sheet I have ever considered as a forerunner of the melancholy catastrophe that so soon afterward happened to our family; and my being caught in it, I believe, was ominous of my preservation from death at the time we were captured.

As I before observed, I got home with my horse very early in the morning, where I found a man who lived in our neighbourhood, and his sister-in-law who had three children, one son and two daughters. I soon learned that they had come there to live a short time; but for what purpose I cannot say. The woman's husband, however, was at that time in Washington's army, fighting for his country; and as her brother-in-law had a house, she had lived with him in his absence. Their names I have forgotten. Immediately after I got home, the man took the horse to go to his own house after a bag of grain, and took his gun in his hand for the purpose of killing some game, if he should chance to see any.

Our family, as usual, were busily employed about their common business. Father was shaving an axe-helve at the side of the house; mother was making preparations for breakfast; my two oldest brothers were at work near the barn: and the little ones, with myself, and the woman and her three children, were in the house.

Breakfast was not yet ready, when we were alarmed by the discharge of a number of guns, that seemed to be near. Mother and the woman before mentioned almost fainted at the report, and every one trembled with fear. On opening the door, the man and horse lay dead near the house, having just been shot by the Indians.

I was afterward informed, that the Indians discovered him at his own house with his gun, and pursued him to father's, where they shot him as I have related. They first secured my father, and then rushed into the house, and without the least resistance made prisoners of my mother, brothers, and sister, the woman, her three children, and myself; and then commenced plundering.

My two brothers, Thomas and John, being at the barn, escaped and went to Virginia, where my grandfather Erwin then lived, as I was informed by a Mr. Fields, who was at my house about the close of the revolutionary war.

The party that took us consisted of six Indians and four Frenchmen, who immediately commenced plundering, as I just observed, and took what they considered most valuable; consisting principally of bread, meal, and meat. Having taken as much provision as they could carry, they set out with their prisoners in great haste, for fear of detection, and soon entered the woods.[1] On our march that day, an Indian went behind us with a whip, with which he frequently lashed the children, to make them keep up. In this manner we travelled till dark, without a mouthful of food or a drop of water, although we had not eaten since the night before. Whenever the little, children cried for water, the Indians would make them drink urine, or go thirsty. At night they encamped in the woods, without fire and without shelter, where we were watched with the greatest vigilance. Extremely fatigued, and very hungry, we were compelled to lie upon the ground, without supper or a drop of water to satisfy the cravings of our appetites.

As in the daytime, so the little ones were made to drink urine in the night, if they cried for water. Fatigue alone brought us a little sleep for the refreshment of our weary limbs; and at the dawn of day we were

---

1. As Mary was born in the year 1742 or 1743, and was taken captive in 1755, she was at this time about thirteen years of age.

again started on our march, in the same order that we had proceeded the day before. About sunrise we were halted, and the Indians gave us a full breakfast of provision that they had brought from my father's house. Each of us, being very hungry, partook of this bounty of the Indians, except father, who was so much overcome with his situation, so much exhausted by anxiety and grief, that silent despair seemed fastened upon his countenance, and he could not be prevailed upon to refresh his sinking nature by the use of a morsel of food. Our repast being finished, we again resumed our march; and before noon passed a small fort, that I heard my father say was called Fort Canagojigge.

That was the only time that I heard him speak from the time we were taken till we were finally separated the following night.

Toward evening, we arrived at the border of a dark and dismal swamp, which was covered with small hemlocks or some other evergreen, and various kinds of bushes, into which we were conducted; and having gone a short distance, we stopped to encamp for the night.

Here we had some bread and meat for supper; but the dreariness of our situation, together with the uncertainty under which we all laboured, as to our future destiny, almost deprived us of the sense of hunger, and destroyed our relish for food.

Mother, from the time we were taken, had manifested a great degree of fortitude, and encouraged us to support our troubles without complaining; and by her conversation, seemed to make the distance and time shorter, and the way more smooth. But father lost all his ambition in the beginning of our trouble, and continued apparently lost to every care—absorbed in melancholy. Here, as before, she insisted on the necessity of our eating; and we obeyed her, but it was done with heavy hearts.

As soon as I had finished my supper,, an Indian took off my shoes and stockings, and put a pair of *moccasins* on my feet, which my mother observed; and believing that they would spare my life, even if they should destroy the other captives, addressed me, as near as I can remember, in the following words:

My dear little Mary. I fear that the time has arrived when we must he parted forever. Your life, my child, I think will be spared; but we shall probably be tomahawked here in this lonesome place by the Indians. Oh! how can I part with you. my darling? What will become of my sweet little Mary? Oh! how can I think of your being continued in captivity, without a hope of your being rescued? Oh! that death had snatched you from my embraces in your infancy: the pain of parting then would have been pleasing to what it now is; and I should have seen the end of your troubles! Alas, my dear! my heart bleeds at the thought of what awaits you; but, if you leave us, remember, my child, your own name, and the names of your father and mother. Be careful and not forget your English tongue. If you shall have an opportunity to get away from the Indians don't try to escape; for if you do they will find and destroy you. Don't forget, my little daughter, the prayers that I have learned you—say them often: be a good child, and God will bless you! May God bless you, my child, and make you comfortable and happy.

During this time, the Indians stripped the shoes and stockings from the little boy that belonged to the woman who was taken with us, and put *moccasins* on his feet, as they had done before on mine. I was crying. An Indian took the little boy and myself by the hand, to lead us off from the company, when my mother exclaimed, "Don't cry, Mary!—don't cry, my child! God will bless you! Farewell—farewell!"

The Indian led us some distance into the bushes or woods, and there lay down with us to spend the night. The recollection of parting with my tender mother kept me awake, while the tears constantly flowed from my eyes. A number of times in the night, the little boy begged of me earnestly to run away with him, and get clear of the Indians; but remembering the advice I had so lately received, and knowing the dangers to which we should be exposed, in travelling without a path and without a guide, through a wilderness unknown to us, I told him that I would not go, and persuaded him to lie still till morning.

Early the next morning, the Indians and Frenchmen that we had left the night before came to us; but our friends were left behind. It is impossible for anyone to form a correct idea of what my feelings were at the sight of those savages, whom I supposed had murdered my parents and brothers, sister and friends, and left them in the swamp, to be devoured by wild beasts! But what could I do? A poor little defenceless girl; without the power or means of escaping; without a home to go to, even if I could be liberated; without a knowledge of the direction or distance to my former place of residence; and without a living friend to whom to fly for protection, I felt a kind of horror, anxiety, and dread, that to me seemed insupportable. I durst not cry—I durst not complain; and to inquire of them the fate of my friends, even if I could have mustered resolution, was beyond my ability, as I could not speak their language, nor they understand mine. My only relief was in silent, stifled sobs.

My suspicions as to the fate of my parents proved too true; for soon after I left them they were killed and scalped, together with Robert, Matthew, Betsey, and the woman and her two children, and mangled in the most shocking manner.

Having given the little boy and myself some bread and meat for breakfast, they led us on as fast as we could travel, and one of them went behind with a long staff, poking up all the grass and weeds that we trailed down by going over them. By taking that precaution, they avoided detection; for each weed was so nicely placed in its natural position, that no one would have suspected that we had passed that way. It is the custom of Indians, when scouting, or on private expeditions, to step carefully, and where no impression of their feet can be left—shunning wet or muddy ground. They seldom take hold of a bush or limb, and never break one; and by observing these precautions, and that of setting up the weeds and grass which they necessarily lop, they completely elude the sagacity of their pursuers, and escape that punishment which they are conscious they merit from the hand of justice.

After a hard day's march we encamped in a thicket, where the Indians made a shelter of boughs, and then built a good fire to warm and dry our benumbed limbs and clothing; for it had rained some through the day. Here we were again fed as before. When the Indians had finished their supper, they took from their baggage a number of scalps, and went about preparing them for the market, or to keep without spoiling, by straining them over small hoops which they prepared for that purpose, and then drying and scraping them by the fire. Having put the scalps, yet wet and bloody, upon the hoops, and stretched them to their full extent, they held them to the fire till they were partly dried, and then, with their knives, commenced scraping off the flesh; and in that way they continued to work, alternately drying and scraping them, till they were dry and clean.

That being done, they combed the hair in the neatest manner, and then painted it and the edges of the scalps, yet on the hoops, red. Those scalps I knew at the time must have been taken from our family, by the colour of the hair. My mother's hair was red; and I could easily distinguish my father's and the children's from each other. That sight was most appalling; yet I was obliged to endure it without complaining. In the course of the night, they made me to understand that they should not have killed the family, if the whites had not pursued them.

Mr. Fields, whom I have before mentioned, informed me that, at the time we were taken, he lived in the vicinity of my father; and that, on hearing of our captivity, the whole neighbourhood turned out in pursuit of the enemy, and to deliver us, if possible; but that their efforts were unavailing. They, however, pursued us to the dark swamp, where they found my father, his family, and companions. stripped, and mangled in the most inhuman manner: that from thence the march of the cruel monsters could not be traced in any direction; and that they returned to their homes with the melancholy tidings of our misfortunes, supposing we had all shared in the massacre.

The next morning we pursued our journey, an Indian going behind us and setting up the weeds, as on the day before. At night, we encamped on the ground in the open air, without a shelter or fire.

In the morning we again set out early, and travelled as on the two former days; though the weather was extremely uncomfortable, from the continual falling of rain and snow.

At night the snow fell fast, and the Indians built a shelter of boughs, and kindled a fire, where we rested tolerably dry through that and the two succeeding nights.

When we stopped, and before the fire was kindled, I was so much fatigued from running, and so far benumbed by the wet and cold, that I expected that I must fall and die before I could get warm and comfortable. The fire, however, soon restored the circulation of blood; and after I had taken my supper, I felt so that I rested well through the night.

On account of the storm, we were two days at that place. On one of those days, a party consisting of six Indians, who had been to the frontier settlements, came to where we were, and brought with them one prisoner—a young white man, who was very tired and dejected. His name I have forgotten.

Misery certainly loves company. I was extremely glad to see him, though I knew from his appearance that his situation was as deplorable as my own, and that he could afford me no kind of assistance. In the afternoon the Indians killed a deer, which they dressed, and then roasted whole; which made them a full meal. We were each allowed a share of their venison, and some bread, so that we made a good meal also.

Having spent three nights and two days at that place, and the storm having ceased, early in the morning the whole company, consisting of twelve Indians, four Frenchmen. the young man, the little boy, and myself, moved on at a moderate pace, without taking the previously-adopted precautions to obliterate or hide our trail.

In the afternoon we came in sight of Fort Du Quesne, (since Fort Pitt, now Pittsburg,) where we halted, while the Indians performed some ceremonies in conformity to their customs on such occasions. That fort was then occupied by the French and Indians. It stood at the junction of the Monongahela, (Falling-in-Banks,) and Alleghany Rivers, where the Ohio River begins to take its name. The word *O-hi-o* signifies bloody.[2]

At the place where we halted, the Indians combed the hair of the young man, the boy, and myself, and then painted our faces and hair red, in the finest Indian style. We were then conducted into the fort, where we received a little bread, and were then shut up in an uninhabited house, and left to tarry alone through the night.

---

2. *O-heé-yo,* the radix of the word Ohio, signifies the "Beautiful River"; and the Iroquoia, by conferring it upon the Alleghany, or head branch of the Ohio, have not only fixed a name from their language upon one of the great rivers of the Continent, but indirectly upon one of the noblest states of our Confederacy.—*League of the Iroquois*

CHAPTER 3

# Mary is Given to Two Seneca Women

The night was spent in gloomy forebodings. What the result of our captivity would be, it was out of our power to determine, or even imagine. At times, we could almost realize the approach of our masters to butcher and scalp us; again, we could nearly see the pile of wood kindled on which we were to be roasted; and then we would imagine ourselves at liberty, alone and defenceless in the forest, surrounded by wild beasts that were ready to devour us. The anxiety of our minds drove sleep from our eyelids; and it was with a dreadful hope and painful impatience that we waited for the morning to determine our fate.

The morning at length arrived, and our masters came early and let us out of the house, and gave the young man and boy to the French, who immediately took them away. Their fate I never learned, as I have not seen nor heard of them since.

I was now left alone in the fort, deprived of my former companions, and of everything that was near or dear to me but life. But it was not long before I was in some measure relieved by the appearance of two pleasant-looking squaws, of the Seneca tribe, who came and examined me attentively for a short time, and then went out. After a few minutes' absence, they returned in company with my former masters, who gave me to the squaws to dispose of as they pleased.

The Indians by whom I was taken were a party of Shawnees,[1] if I

1. The home country of the Shawnees, at the period of colonization by the Europeans, was in the western part of the present state of Kentucky. They are thus located by Albert Gallatin, on his map of the sites of the Indian tribes of the Continent, published in the second volume of the *Transactions of the American Ethnological Society*. The name of this nation in the Seneca dialect of the Iroquois language is *Sa-wä-nó-o-no*.

MARY BEING ARRAYED IN INDIAN COSTUME.

remember right, that lived, when at home, a long distance down the Ohio.

My former Indian masters and the two squaws were soon ready to leave the fort, and accordingly embarked—the Indians in a large canoe, and the two squaws and myself in a small one—and went down the Ohio. When we set off, an Indian in the forward canoe took the scalps of my former friends, strung them on a pole that he placed upon his shoulder, and in that manner carried them, standing in the stern of the canoe directly before us, as we sailed down the river, to the town where the two squaws resided.

On the way we passed a Shawnee town, where I saw a number of heads, arms, legs, and other fragments of the bodies of some white people who had just been burned. The parts that remained were hanging on a pole, which was supported at each end by a crotch stuck in the ground, and were roasted or burnt black as a coal. The fire was yet burning; and the whole appearance afforded a spectacle so shocking that even to this day the blood almost curdles in my veins when I think of them.

At night we arrived at a small Seneca Indian town, at the mouth of a small river that was called by the Indians, in the Seneca language, *She-nan-jee*,[2] about eighty miles by water from the fort, where the two squaws to whom I belonged resided. There we landed, and the Indians went on; which was the last I ever saw of them.

Having made fast to the shore, the squaws left me in the canoe while they went to their *wigwam* or house in the town, and returned with a suit of Indian clothing, all new, and very clean and nice. My clothes, though whole and good when I was taken, were now torn in pieces, so that I was almost naked. They first undressed me, and threw my rags into the river; then washed me clean and dressed me in the new suit they had just brought, in complete Indian style; and then led me home and me in the centre of their *wigwam*.

I had been in that situation but a few minutes before all the squaws in the town came in to see me. I was soon surrounded by them, and they immediately setup a most dismal howling, crying bitterly, and wringing their hands in all the agonies of grief for a deceased rela-

---

2. That town, according to the geographical description given by Mrs. Jemison, must have stood at the mouth of Indian Cross Creek, which is about 76 miles by water, below Pittsburgh; or at the mouth of Indian Short Creek, 87 miles below Pittsburgh, where the town of Warren now stands: But at which of those places I am unable to determine.—Author

tive.

Their tears flowed freely, and they exhibited all the signs of real mourning. At the commencement of this scene, one of their number began, in a voice somewhat between speaking and singing, to recite some words to the following purport, and continued the recitation till the ceremony was ended; the company at the same time varying the appearance of their countenances, gestures, and tone of voice, so as to correspond with the sentiments expressed by their leader.

Oh our brother! Alas! He is dead—he has gone; he will never return! Friendless he died on the field of the slain, where his bones are yet lying unburied! Oh, who will not mourn his sad fate? No tears dropped around him; oh, no! No tears of his sisters were there! He fell in his prime, when his arm was most needed to keep us from danger! Alas! he has gone! and left us in sorrow, his loss to bewail: Oh where is his spirit? His spirit went naked, and hungry it wanders, and thirsty and wounded it groans to return! Oh helpless and wretched, our brother has gone! No blanket nor food to nourish and warm him; nor candles to light him, nor weapons of war:—Oh, none of those comforts had he! But well we remember his deeds!—The deer he could take on the chase!

The panther shrunk back at the sight of his strength! His enemies fell at his feet! He was brave and courageous in war! As the fawn was harmless: his friendship was ardent: his temper was gentle: his pity was great! Oh! our friend, our companion is dead! Our brother, your brother, alas! he is gone! But why do we grieve for his loss? In the strength of a warrior, undaunted he left us, to fight by the side of the Chiefs! His war-whoop was shrill! His rifle well aimed laid his enemies low: his tomahawk drank of their blood: and his knife flayed their scalps while yet covered with gore!

And why do we mourn? Though he fell on the field of the slain, with glory he fell, and his spirit went up to the land of his fathers in war! Then why do we mourn? With transports of joy they received him, and fed him, and clothed him, and welcomed him there! Oh friends, he is happy; then dry up your tears! His spirit has seen our distress, and sent us a helper whom with pleasure we greet. Deh-he-wä-mis has come: then let us receive her with joy!—She is handsome and pleasant! Oh! she is our sister, and gladly we welcome her here. In the place of our brother she stands in our tribe. With care we will guard her from trouble; and may she be happy till her spirit shall leave us.

In the course of that ceremony, from mourning they became serene—joy sparkled in their countenances, and they seemed to rejoice over me as over a long lost child. I was made welcome amongst them as a sister to the two Squaws before mentioned, and was called Deh-he-wä-mis; which being interpreted, signifies a pretty girl, a handsome girl, or a pleasant, good thing. That is the name by which I have ever since been called by the Indians.

I afterwards learned that the ceremony I at that time passed through, was that of adoption. The two squaws had lost a brother in Washington's war, sometime in the year before and in consequence of his death went up to Fort Pitt, on the day on which I arrived there, in order to receive a prisoner or an enemy's scalp, to supply their loss. It is a custom of the Indians, when one of their number is slain or taken prisoner in battle, to give to the nearest relative to the dead or absent, a prisoner, if they have chanced to take one, and if not, to give him the scalp of an enemy. On the return of the Indians from conquest, which is always announced by peculiar shoutings, demonstrations of joy, and the exhibition of some trophy of victory, the mourners come forward and make their claims. If they receive a prisoner, it is at their option either to satiate their vengeance by taking his life in the most cruel manner they can conceive of; or, to receive and adopt him into the family, in the place of him whom they have lost. All the prisoners that are taken in battle and carried to the encampment or town by the Indians, are given to the bereaved families, till their number is made good.

And unless the mourners have but just received the news of their bereavement, and are under the operation of a paroxysm of grief, anger and revenge; or, unless the prisoner is very old, sickly, or homely, they generally save him, and treat him kindly. But if their mental wound is fresh, their loss so great that they deem it irreparable, or if their prisoner or prisoners do not meet their approbation, no torture, let it be ever so cruel, seems sufficient to make them satisfaction. It is family, and not national, sacrifices amongst the Indians, that has given them an indelible stamp as barbarians, and identified their character with the idea which is generally formed of unfeeling ferocity, and the most barbarous cruelty.

It was my happy lot to be accepted for adoption; and at the time of the ceremony I was received by the two squaws, to supply the place of their brother in the family; and I was ever considered and treated by them as a real sister, the same as though I had been born of their mother.

During my adoption, I sat motionless, nearly terrified to death at the appearance and actions of the company, expecting every moment to feel their vengeance, and suffer death on the spot. I was, however, happily disappointed, when at the close of the ceremony the company retired, and my sisters went about employing every means for my consolation and comfort.[3]

Being now settled and provided with a home, I was employed in nursing the children, and doing light work about the house. Occasionally I was sent out with the Indian hunters, when they went but a short distance, to help them carry their game.

My situation was easy; I had no particular hardships to endure. But still, the recollection of my parents, my brothers and sisters, my

---

3. "The Iroquois never exchanged prisoners with Indian nations, nor ever sought to reclaim their own people from captivity among them. Adoption or the torture were the alternative chances of the captive. . . . . . A regular ceremony of adoption was performed in each case to complete the naturalization. With captives this ceremony was the gauntlet, after which new names were assigned to them. Upon the return of a war party with captives, if they had lost any of their own number in the expedition, the families to which these belonged were first allowed an opportunity to supply from the captives the places made vacant in their household. Any family could then adopt out of the residue any such as chanced to attract their favourable notice, or whom they wished to save. At the time appointed, the women and children of the village arranged themselves in two parallel rows just without the village, each one having a whip with which to lash the captives as they pawed between the lines. The male captives, who alone were required to undergo this test of their powers of endurance, were brought out, and each one was shown in turn the house in which he was to take refuge, and which was to be his future home if he passed successfully through the ordeal. They were then taken to the head of this long avenue of whips, and were compelled, one after another, to run through it for their lives, and for the entertainment of the surrounding throng, exposed at every step, undefended, and with naked backs, to the merciless infliction of the whip. Those who fell from exhaustion were immediately dispatched, as unworthy to be saved; but those who emerged in safety from this test of their physical energies were from that moment treated with the utmost affection and kindness. When the perils of the gauntlet were over, the captive ceased to be an enemy, and became an Iroquois. Not only so, but he was received into the family by which he was adopted, with all the cordiality of affection, and into all the relations of the one whose place he was henceforth to occupy."—*League of the Iroquois*.

home, and my own captivity, destroyed my happiness, and made me constantly solitary, lonesome and gloomy.

My sisters would not allow me to speak English in their hearing; but remembering the charge that my dear mother gave me at the time I left her, whenever I chanced to be alone I made a business of repeating my prayer, catechism, or something I had learned in order that I might not forget my own language. By practising in that way I retained it till I came to Genesee flats, where I soon became acquainted with English people with whom I have been almost daily in the habit of conversing.

My sisters were diligent in teaching me their language; and to their great satisfaction I soon learned so that I could understand it readily, and speak it fluently. I was very fortunate in falling into their hands; for they were kind good natured women; peaceable and mild in their dispositions; temperate and decent in their habits, and very tender and gentle towards me. I have great reason to respect them, though they have been dead a great number of years.

The town where they lived was pleasantly situated on the Ohio, at the mouth of the Shenanjee: the land produced good corn; the woods furnished a plenty of game, and the waters abounded with fish. Another river emptied itself into the Ohio, directly opposite the mouth of the Shenanjee. We spent the summer at that place, where we planted, hoed, and harvested a large crop of corn, of an excellent quality.

About the time of corn harvest, Fort Pitt was taken from the French by the English. [4]

The corn being harvested, the Indians took it on horses and in canoes, and proceeded down the Ohio, occasionally stopping to hunt a few days, till we arrived at the mouth of Sciota River; where they established their winter quarters, and continued hunting till the ensuing spring, in the adjacent wilderness. While at that place I went with the other children to assist the hunters to bring in their game. The

---

4. The above statement is apparently an error; and is to be attributed solely to the treachery of the old lady's memory; though she is confident that that event took place at the time above mentioned. It is certain that Fort Pitt was not evacuated by the French and given up to the English, till sometime in November, 1758. It is possible, however, that an armistice was agreed upon, and that for a time, between the spring of 1755 and 1758, both nations visited that post without fear of molestation. As the succeeding part of the narrative corresponds with the true historical chain of events, the public will overlook this circumstance, which appears unsupported by history.—Author.

forests on the Sciota were well stocked with elk, deer, and other large animals; and the marshes contained large numbers of beaver, muskrat, &c. which made excellent hunting for the Indians; who depended, for their meat, upon their success in taking elk and deer; and for ammunition and clothing, upon the beaver, muskrat, and other furs that they could take in addition to their peltry.

The season for hunting being passed, we all returned in the spring to the mouth of the river Shenanjee, to the houses and fields we had left in the fall before. There we again planted our corn, squashes, and beans, on the fields that we occupied the preceding summer.

About planting time, our Indians all went up to Fort Pitt, to make peace with the British, and took me with them.[5] We landed on the opposite side of the river from the fort, and encamped for the night. Early the next morning the Indians took me over to the fort to see the white people that were there. It was then that my heart bounded to be liberated from the Indians and to be restored to my friends and my country. The white people were surprised to see me with the Indians, enduring the hardships of a savage life, at so early an age, and with so delicate a constitution as I appeared to possess. They asked me my name; where and when I was taken, and appeared very much interested on my behalf. They were continuing their inquiries, when my sisters became alarmed, believing that I should be taken from them, hurried me into their canoe and recrossed the river—took their bread out of the fire and fled with me, without stopping, till they arrived at the river Shenanjee. So great was their fear of losing me, or of my being given up in the treaty, that they never once stopped rowing till they got home.

Shortly after we left the shore opposite the fort, as I was informed by one of my Indian brothers, the white people came over to take me back; but after considerable inquiry, and having made diligent search to find where I was hid, they returned with heavy hearts. Although I had then been with the Indians something over a year, and had become considerably habituated to their mode of living, and attached to my sisters, the sight of white people who could speak English inspired me with an unspeakable anxiety to go home with them, and share in the blessings of civilization. My sudden departure and escape from them, seemed like a second captivity, and for a long time I brooded

---

5. History is silent as to any treaty having been made between the English, and French and Indians, at that time; though it is possible that a truce was agreed upon, and that the parties met for the purpose of concluding a treaty of peace.

the thoughts of my miserable situation with almost as much sorrow and dejection as I had done those of my first sufferings. Time, the destroyer of every affection, wore away my unpleasant feelings, and I became as contented as before.

We tended our cornfields through the summer; and after we had harvested the crop, we again went down the river to the hunting ground on the Sciota, where we spent the winter, as we had done the winter before.

Early in the spring we sailed up the Ohio River, to a place that the Indians called *Wi-ish-to*,[6] where one river emptied into the Ohio on one side, and another on the other. At that place the Indians built a town, and we planted corn.

We lived three summers at Wiishto, and spent each winter on the Sciota.

The first summer of our living at Wiishto, a party of Delaware Indians came up the river, took up their residence, and lived in common with us. They brought five white prisoners with them, who by their conversation, made my situation much more agreeable, as they could all speak English. I have forgotten the names of all of them except one, which was Priscilla Ramsay. She was a very handsome, good natured girl, and was married soon after she came to Wiishto to Captain Little Billy's uncle, who went with her on a visit to her friends in the states. Having tarried with them as long as she wished to, she returned with her husband to Can-a-ah-tua, where he died. She, after his death, married a white man by the name of Nettles, and now lives with him (if she is living) on Grand River, Upper Canada.

Not long after the Delawares came to live with us, at Wiishto, my sisters told me that I must go and live with one of them, whose name was *She-nin-jee*. Not daring to cross them, or disobey their commands, with a great degree of reluctance I went; and Sheninjee and I were married according to Indian custom.

Sheninjee was a noble man—large in stature; elegant in his appearance; generous in his conduct; courageous in war; a friend to peace, and a great lover of justice. He supported a degree of dignity far above his rank, and merited and received the confidence and friendship of all the tribes with whom he was acquainted. Yet, Sheninjee was an Indian. The idea of spending my days with him, at first seemed perfectly ir-

---

6. Wiishto I suppose was situated near the mouth of Indian Guyundat, 327 miles below Pittsburgh, and 73 above Big Sciota; or at the mouth of Swan Creek, 307 miles below Pittsburgh.

reconcilable to my feelings: but his good nature, generosity, tenderness, and friendship towards me, soon gained my affection; and, strange as it may seem, I loved him! To me he was ever kind in sickness, and always treated me with gentleness; in fact, he was an agreeable husband, and a comfortable companion.

We lived happily together till the time of our final separation, which happened two or three years after our marriage, as I shall presently relate.

In the second summer of my living at Wiishto, I had a child at the time that the kernels of corn first appeared on the cob. When I was taken sick, Sheninjee was absent, and I was sent to a small shed, on the bank of the river, which was made of boughs, where I was obliged to stay till my husband returned. My two sisters, who were my only companions, attended me, and on the second day of my confinement my child was born but it lived only two days. It was a girl: and notwithstanding the shortness of the time that I possessed it, it was a great grief to me to lose it.

After the birth of my child, I was very sick, but was not allowed to go into the house for two weeks; when, to my great joy, Sheninjee returned, and I was taken in and as comfortably provided for as our situation would admit of. My disease continued to increase for a number of days; and I became so far reduced that my recovery was despaired of by my friends, and I concluded that my troubles would soon be finished. At length, however, my complaint took a favourable turn, and by the time that the corn was ripe I was able to get about. I continued to gain my health, and in the fall was able to go to our winter quarters, on the Saratoga, with the Indians.

From that time, nothing remarkable occurred to me till the fourth winter of my captivity, when I had a son born, while I was at Sciota: I had a quick recovery, and my child was healthy. To commemorate the name of my much lamented father, I called my son Thomas Jemison.

# CHAPTER 4

# Removal from Wi-ish-to
# to the Genesee

In the spring, when Thomas was three or four moons [months] old, we returned from Sciota to Wiishto, and soon after set out to go to Fort Pitt, to dispose of our fur and skins, that we had taken in the winter, and procure some necessary articles for the use of our family.

I had then been with the Indians four summers and four winters, and had become so far accustomed to their mode of living, habits and dispositions, that my anxiety to get away, to be set at liberty, and leave them, had almost subsided. With them was my home; my family was there, and there I had many friends to whom I was warmly attached in consideration of the favours, affection and friendship with which they had uniformly treated me, from the time of my adoption.

Our labour was not severe; and that of one year was exactly similar, in almost every respect, to that of the others, without that endless variety that is to be observed in the common labour of the white people. Notwithstanding the Indian women have all the fuel and bread to procure, and the cooking to perform, their task is probably not harder than that of white women, who have those articles provided for them; and their cares certainly are not half as numerous, nor as great. In the summer season, we planted, tended and harvested our corn, and generally had all our children with us; but had no master to oversee or drive us, so that we could work as leisurely as we pleased. We had no ploughs on the Ohio; but performed the whole process of planting and hoeing with a small tool that resembled, in some respects, a hoe with a very short handle.

We pursued our farming business according to the general custom of Indian women, which is as follows: In order to expedite their business, and at the same time enjoy each other's company, they all work together in one field, or at whatever job they may have on hand. In the spring, they choose an old active squaw to be their driver and overseer, when at labour, for the ensuing year. She accepts the honour, and they consider themselves bound to obey her.

When the time for planting arrives, and the soil is prepared, the squaws are assembled in the morning, and conducted into a field, where each plants one row. They then go into the next field and plant once across, and so on till they have gone through the tribe. If any remains to be planted, they again commence where they did at first, (in the same field,) and so keep on till the whole is finished. By this rule, they perform their labour of every kind, and every jealousy of one having done more or less than another is effectually avoided.

Each squaw cuts, her own wood; but it is all brought to the house under the direction of the overseer.

Their method of computing time was by moons and winters: a moon is a month; and the time from the end of one winter to that of another, a year.

From sunset till sunrise, they say that the sun is asleep. In the old of the moon, when it does not shine in the night, they say it is dead. They rejoice greatly at the sight of the new moon.

In order to commemorate great events, and preserve the chronology of them, the war chief in each tribe keeps a war-post. This post is a peeled stick of timber ten or twelve feet high, that is erected in the town. For a campaign, they make, or rather the chief makes, a perpendicular red mark, about three inches long and half an inch wide; on the opposite side from this, for a scalp, they make a red cross, thus, +; on another side, for a prisoner taken alive, they make a red cross in this manner, **X**, with a head, or dot; and by placing such significant hieroglyphics in so conspicuous a situation, they are enabled to ascertain with great certainty the time and circumstances of past events.

Hiokatoo had a war-post, on which was recorded his military exploits, and other things that he thought worth preserving.

Our cooking consisted in pounding our corn into *samp* or *hominy*, boiling the *hominy*, making now and then a cake and baking it in the ashes, and in boiling or roasting our venison. As our cooking and eating utensils consisted of a *hominy* block and pestle, a small kettle, a knife or two, and a few vessels of bark or wood, it required but little time to keep them in order for use.

Spinning, weaving, sewing, stocking knitting, and the like, are arts which have never been practised in the Indian tribes generally. After the revolutionary war, I learned to sew, so that I could make my own clothing after a poor fashion; but the other domestic arts I have been wholly ignorant of the application of, since my captivity. In the season of hunting, it was our business, in addition to our cooking, to bring home the game that was taken by the Indians, dress it, and carefully preserve the eatable meat, and prepare or dress the skins. Our clothing was fastened together with strings of deer skin, and tied on with the same.

In that manner we lived, without any of those jealousies, quarrels, and revengeful battles between families and individuals, which have been common in the Indian tribes since the introduction of ardent spirits amongst them.

The use of ardent spirits amongst the Indians, and the attempts which have been made to civilize and Christianize them by the white people, has constantly made them worse and worse; increased their vices, and robbed them of many of their virtues; and will ultimately produce their extermination. I have seen, in a number of instances, the effects of education upon some of our Indians, who were taken when young, from their families, and placed at school before they had had an opportunity to contract many Indian habits, and there kept till they arrived to manhood; but I have never seen one of those but what was an Indian in every respect after he returned. Indians must and will be Indians, In spite of all the means that can be used for their cultivation in the sciences and arts.

One thing only marred my happiness, while I lived with them on the Ohio; and that was the recollection that I had once had tender parents, and a home that I loved. Aside from that consideration, or, if I had been taken in infancy, I should have been contented in my situation. Notwithstanding all that has been said against the Indians, in consequence of their cruelties to their enemies—cruelties that I have witnessed, and had abundant proof of—it is a fact that they are naturally kind, tender and peaceable towards their friends, and strictly honest; and that those cruelties have been practised, only upon their enemies, according to their idea of justice.

At the time we left Wiishto, it was impossible for me to suppress a sigh of regret on parting with those who had truly been my friends—with those whom I had every reason to respect. On account of a part of our family living at Genishau, or Genesee, we thought it doubtful whether we should return directly from Pittsburgh, or go from thence on a visit to see them.

Our company consisted of my husband, my two Indian brothers, my little son and myself. We embarked in a canoe that was large enough to contain ourselves, and our effects, and proceeded on our voyage up the river.

Nothing remarkable occurred to us on our way, till we arrived at the mouth of a creek which Sheninjee and my brother said was the outlet of Sandusky Lake; where, as they said, two or three English traders in fur and skins had kept a trading house but a short time before, though they were then absent. We had passed the trading house but a short distance, when we met three white men floating down the river, with the appearance of having been recently murdered by the Indians, we supposed them to be the bodies of the traders, whose store we had passed the same day. Sheninjee being alarmed for fear of being apprehended as one of the murderers, if he should go on, resolved to put about immediately, and we accordingly returned to where the traders had lived, and there landed.

At the trading house we found a party of Shawnee Indians, who had taken a young white man prisoner, and had just begun to torture him for the sole purpose of gratifying their curiosity in exulting at his distress. They at first made him stand up, while they slowly pared his ears and split them into strings; they then made a number of slight incisions in his face; and then bound him upon the ground, rolled him in the dirt, and rubbed it in his wounds: some of them at the same time whipping him with small rods! The poor fellow cried for mercy and yelled most piteously.

The sight of his distress seemed too much for me to endure: I begged of them to desist—I entreated them with tears to release him. At length they attended to my intercessions, and set him at liberty. He was shockingly disfigured, bled profusely, and appeared to be in great pain: but as soon as he was liberated he made off in haste, which was the last I saw of him.

We soon learned that the same party of Shawnees had, but a few hours before, massacred the three white traders whom we saw in the river, and had plundered their store. We, however, were not molested by them, and after a short stay at that place, moved up the creek about forty miles to a Shawnee town, which the Indians called Gaw-gush-shaw-ga,[1] (which being interpreted signifies a mask or a false face.)

1. *Gä-gó-sa*, in the Seneca dialect, signifies "a False face," and *Gä-gó-sa-ga* "the place of the false face," which is doubtless the correct orthography of this word.

The creek that we went up was called Candusky. It was now summer; and having tarried a few days at Gawgushshawga, we moved on up the creek to a place that was called Yis-kah-wa-na, (meaning in English open mouth.)

As I have before observed, the family to which I belonged was part of a tribe of Seneca Indians, who lived, at that time, at a place called Genishau, from the name of the tribe, that was situated on a river of the same name which is now called Genesee. The word Genishau signifies a shining, clear or open place.[2] Those of us who lived on the Ohio, had frequently received invitations from those at Genishau, by one of my brothers, who usually went and returned every season, to come and live with them, and my two sisters had been gone almost two years.

While we were at Yiskahwana, my brother arrived there from Genishau, and insisted so strenuously upon our going home (as he called it) with him, that my two brothers concluded to go, and to take me with them.

By this time the summer was gone, and the time for harvesting corn had arrived. My brothers, for fear of the rainy season setting in early, thought it best to set out immediately that we might have good travelling. Sheninjee consented to have me go with my brothers; but concluded to go down the river himself with some fur and skins which he had on hand, spend the winter in hunting with his friends, and come to me in the spring following.

That was accordingly agreed upon, and he set out for Wiishto; and my three brothers and myself, with my little son on my back, at the same time set out for Genishau. We came on to Upper Sandusky, to an Indian town that we found deserted by its inhabitants, in consequence of their having recently murdered some English traders, who resided amongst them. That town was owned and had been occupied by Delaware Indians, who, when they left it, buried their provision in the earth, in order to preserve it from their enemies, or to have a supply for themselves if they should chance to return. My brothers understood the customs of the Indians when they were obliged to fly from their enemies; and suspecting that their corn at least must have been hid, made diligent search, and at length found a large quantity of it, together with beans, sugar and honey, so carefully buried that it was

---

2. *Gen-nis-he-yo* is the true spelling. It signifies "the beautiful valley," from which the river takes its name. The adjective *we-yo*, which means "grand", or "beautiful", is incorporated in the word, and thus determines its signification.

completely dry and as good as when they left it.

As our stock of provision was scanty, we considered ourselves extremely fortunate in finding so seasonable a supply, with so little trouble. Having caught two or three horses, that we found there, and furnished ourselves with a good store of food, we travelled on till we came to the mouth of French Creek, where we hunted two days, and from thence came on to Conowongo Creek, where we were obliged to stay seven or ten days, in consequence of our horses having left us and straying into the woods. The horses, however, were found, and we again prepared to resume our journey. During our stay at that place the rain fell fast, and had raised the creek to such a height that it was seemingly impossible for us to cross it. A number of times we ventured in, but were compelled to return, barely escaping with our lives. At length we succeeded in swimming our horses and reached the opposite shore; though I but just escaped with my little boy from being drowned. From Sandusky the path that we travelled was crooked and obscure; but was tolerably well understood by my oldest brother, who had travelled it a number of times, when going to and returning from the Cherokee wars.

The fall by this time was considerably advanced, and the rains, attended with cold winds, continued daily to increase the difficulties of travelling. From Conowongo we came to a place, called by the Indians Che-ua-shung-gau-tau, and from that to U-na-waum-gwa, (which means an eddy, not strong), where the early frosts had destroyed the corn so that the Indians were in danger of starving for the want of bread. Having rested ourselves two days at that place, we came on to Caneadea[3] and stayed one day, and then continued our march till we arrived at Genishau. Genishau at that time was a large Seneca town, thickly inhabited, lying on Genesee River, opposite what is now called the Free Ferry, adjoining Fall-Brook, and about south west of the present village of Geneseo, the county seat for the county of Livingston, in the state of New-York.

Those only who have travelled on foot the distance of five or six hundred miles, through an almost pathless wilderness, can form an idea of the fatigue and sufferings that I endured on that journey. My clothing was thin and illy calculated to defend me from the continually drenching rains with which I was daily completely wet, and at night with nothing but my wet blanket to cover me, I had to sleep

---

3. Caneadea is well-preserved Seneca name. The original *Gä-ó-yä-de-o*, signifies "where the heavens rest upon the earth."

on the naked ground, and generally without a shelter, save such as nature had provided. In addition to all that, I had to carry my child, then about nine months old, every step of the journey on my back, or in my arms, and provide for his comfort and prevent his suffering, as far as my poverty of means would admit. Such was the fatigue that I sometimes felt, that I thought it impossible for me to go through, and I would almost abandon the idea of even trying to proceed. My brothers were attentive, and at length, as I have stated, we reached our place of destination, in good health, and without having experienced a day's sickness from the time we left Yiskahwana.

We were kindly received by my Indian mother and the other members of the family, who appeared to make me welcome; and my two sisters, whom I had not seen in two years, received me with every expression of love and friendship, and that they really felt what they expressed, I have never had the least reason to doubt. The warmth of their feelings, the kind reception which I met with, and the continued favours' that I received at their hands, riveted my affection for them so strongly that I am constrained to believe that I loved them as I should have loved my own sister had she lived, and I had been brought up with her.

# The Genesee Valley

Having conducted the principal subject of our narrative to Gen-ishau, or Little Beard's Town,[2] on the banks of Genesee River, wher-eon, within the space of twelve miles along that stream, she has since resided seventy-two years of her life—this likewise being the ground on which most of the scenes we are about to relate, whether of joy or sorrow, pleasure or pain, whether ludicrous or horrible, were enact-ed—we will give the reader a brief geographical sketch of the country, and point out the localities, and those in the surrounding country, most of which have already been, or will hereafter be, referred to in this narrative.

It will be understood, that, in describing Indian villages, etc., we have relation to their state then; for some of them have long since been deserted by the Indians, and demolished by the whites; and at this time, 1842, all those on the Genesee River have ceased to exist, scarce leaving a memorial or trace to point out the spot on which they stood. It will likewise be observed that the distances herein given are according to the Indian trails or paths usually travelled by them in that early day.

A few remarks on Indian names and the Indian language, in this place, may be serviceable to the reader who is unacquainted with the significant properties of Indian proper names, and the monotonous sounds and full aspirations of the language of the Iroquois. It has been often observed that a great discrepancy exists among writers, not only in the spelling, but in the necessary pronunciation of Indian names

---

1. This chapter was added by Ebenezer Mix, Esq.
2. The name of Little Beard's Town was *De-o-nún-dä-gä-a*, signifying "Where the hill is near." It was situated upon the west side of the Genesee Valley, immediately in front of Cuylerville.

of the same persons or places. It requires but a short explanation to elucidate, the cause of this difficulty. Among the Six Nations, not only each nation converses in a different dialect, but each tribe in the same nation have peculiarities in their language not common in the other tribes, although probably not varying more than the dialects in many of the Bounties in England.

All Indian names, whether of persons or places, are significant of some supposed quality, appearance, or local situation; and the Indians having no written language originally, denominated persons and places in conformity to such quality, etc., in their own dialect.

The better to understood, we will mention a particular cast or two, which will give a full explanation to the position assumed: Red Jacket, the celebrated Indian orator, had six or seven different, and in some instances very dissimilar Indian names, as written or spoken; but they all meant, in the dialect to which they belonged, "Keeper Awake." The same remarks will apply to the name of the creek which empties into Genesee River, near Mount Morris, generally called Canniskrauga,[3] which has four or five other quite different Indian names, all meaning the same, in English, to wit, "Among the slippery-elms," as the creek bore the name of an Indian village through which it passed, the village having been named from its local situation.

These explanations were obtained some years since, from the late Captain Horatio Jones, who was one of the best, if not the best Indian linguist in the country his explanation had an influential bearing in an important land trial, as that creek had been called by several very different Indian names in the old title-deeds of large tracts of land. In order to have a correct idea of the pronunciation of Indian names, they must be divided into as many monosyllabical words as there are syllables, for so they originally were, and an *h* added to almost every syllable ending with a vowel. Therefore, as is the case in the pronunciation of all sentences composed of words of one syllable only, all difference of accent is destroyed, and the Indians use very little difference of emphasis. For example, take the original name of Canandaigua, as now spelled and pronounced in the Seneca language, Cah-nan-dah-gwah.[4]

Formerly, in using Indian names, it was necessary to pay some at-

---

3. The name by which this creek and the village of Dansville is now known to the Senecas is, *Gä-mis-ga-go*, signifying, "among the milkweed."
4. *Gä-nún-da-gwa*, "a place selected for a settlement," is the present spelling and pronunciation of this name.

tention to the Indian pronunciation, so as to be understood by the aborigines; but as they, together with their languages, are fast fading from among us, that necessity no longer exists. Therefore, it becomes necessary to Anglicise such names, and make them conform to the English pronunciation in as soft and smooth sounds as possible, to which the letters composing the word, when written, should be made to correspond.

Little Beard's Town, where Mary Jemison first resided when she came to Genesee River, was the most considerable Indian village, or town, in its vicinity. We have no means at this time of ascertaining, or even estimating, its extent or population; but tradition, as well as Mary Jemison, informs us, that it covered a large territory for a village, and that it was thickly populated.

Its chief, or ruler, was Little Beard—a strong-minded, ambitious, and cruel man; and an arbitrary and despotic ruler.

This village stood near the north end of the twelve miles in length heretofore mentioned, on the Genesee Flats, on the west side of the river, between the present villages of Genesee and Moscow, about midway, although nearest to Moscow, and near the site of the new village of Cuyler, on the Genesee Valley Canal.

The tract of country around its site has the most delightful appearance imaginable, considering there are no lofty snow-clad peaks, deafening cataracts, or unfathomable dells, to stamp it with the appellation of romantic. The alluvial flats through which the river meanders for four or five miles above and many miles below are from one mile to two miles wide, as level as a placid lake, and as fertile, to say the least, as any land in this state. Thousands of acres of these flats were cleared of their timber when Indian tradition commences their description. These flats are encompassed on each side by a rolling country, gradually rising as it recedes from the river, but in no place so abrupt as to merit the cognomen of a hill.

This was the terrestrial paradise of the Senecas; and to this tract they gave the name of Gen-ish-a-u, Chen-ne-se-co, Gen-ne-se-o, or Gen-ne-see, as pronounced by the different Indian tribes, and being interpreted, all meaning substantially the same; to wit, Shining-Clear-Opening, Pleasant-Clear-Opening, Clear-Valley, or Pleasant-Open-Valley. From this favourite spot Genesee River took its name; and these flats, at that early period, assumed and still continue to retain exclusively the, name of Genesee Flats, as a distinction from Gardeau, Caneadea, and other flats which bear local names although lying on the same river.

Genesee River rises in Pennsylvania, and, after entering this state, pursues its course with some rapidity, a little west of north, through a hilly country, forming little, if any, alluvial flats, until it approaches Belvidere, (Judge Church's villa near Angelica,) about twenty miles from Pennsylvania line. Front thence it continues the same general course with less rapidity, winding its way through flats of a greater or less width, to a point in Caneadea, about thirty-three miles from Pennsylvania line, following the general course of the river, where it alters to east of north, which direction it pursues until it falls into Lake Ontario. From Belvidere to this bow, or rather angle in the river, and from the angle to the falls below Portageville, the flats are enclosed on each side by high lands, although not precipitous or lofty. The river continues to run with moderate rapidity through flats from this angle to near Portageville, where the highlands close in to the river banks.

At Portageville, about fifteen miles from the angle at Caneadea, begin the great Portage Falls in this river. From the upper falls to Mount Morris and Squawkie Hill, a distance of sixteen miles, the river rims through a chasm, the sides of which are, the greater part of the distance, formed by solid, and almost, or quite, perpendicular walls of rock, from two to four hundred feet high. In some places, however, these walls diverge so far from each other as to allow spots of excellent alluvial flats to be formed on one side of the river or the other, and in some places on both.

Immediately above the upper falls there exists all the appearance of a ridge-of rock having once run across the river, in which case it would have raised the water some two hundred feet above its present level, and, of course, formed a lake from one to two miles wide, and extending back over the Caneadea and other flats, to Belvidere, distance of twenty-eight or thirty miles; but, if ever this was the case, the river has, centuries ago, cut through this ridge, and formed considerable rapids where it stood, above and opposite Portageville. The river, after apparently cutting through this ridge, precipitates itself into the chasm below, by a somewhat broken, although what would be termed perpendicular fall of sixty-six feet. The stream at this place is about twelve rods wide, after which it flows through the chasm on a smooth rock bottom. Half a mile below the upper falls, the river, (where it is about fifteen rods wide,) again precipitates itself in an unbroken sheet, one hundred and ten feet perpendicularly into a deeper channel, forming the "Middle Falls."

The magnificence and beauty of these falls is not exceeded by any thing of the kind in the state, except the cataract of Niagara. On the west side of the river, at the top of the falls, is a small flat piece of land, or rather rock, on which is a saw-mill and several dwelling houses, which can be approached, down a ravine from the west, with any kind of carriage. The stream pursues its course in the same direction, pent within its rock-bound and precipitous shores, about two miles, where it takes its third and last leap in this vicinity, of ninety-three feet, into a still deeper chasm, the greater body of water falling on the eastern side, where a portion of it falls into a kind of hanging rock basin, about one-third of the distance down, and then takes another leap. This fall can be approached on the east side by pedestrians with perfect safety.

The river then pursues its north-eastern course, through its deep and narrow channel, to Gardeau Flats, about five miles from the lower falls. The banks of the river, or rather the land bordering on the chasm the greater portion of this distance, is covered with elegant white and Norway pine. At the upper end of the Gardeau Flats is the Great Slide, which has been so often noticed as a great curiosity.

In the month of May, 1817, a portion of the land on the west side of the river, thickly covered with heavy timber, suddenly gave way, and with a tremendous crash slid into the bed of the river, which is so completely filled that the stream formed a new channel on the east side of it, where it continues to run. This slide, as it now lies, contains twenty-two acres, and has a considerable share of the timber that formerly covered it still standing erect and growing, although it has suffered the shock produced by a fall of some two hundred feet below its former elevation.

The Gardeau Flats are from eighty to one hundred and twenty rods wide, and extend two miles and a quarter down the river, lying mostly on the west side of it. There are several ravines and depressions in the high banks on both sides of the river at the upper end of these flats, so that a road has been made which admits the passage of carriages from the highlands on one side of the river to the highlands on the other, a bridge having been erected across the river: this place above the slide is called St. Helena. Some four miles below St. Helena is Smoky Hollow, containing from two to three hundred acres alluvial flats, approachable from the west only with safety, and in that direction through a ravine and down a steep declivity: this was within Mrs. Jemison's original reservation.

Below this place three or four miles, the river receives .the outlet of Silver Lake.[5] This lake or pond is a beautiful pellucid sheet of water, three and a half miles long, and from half to three-fourths of a mile in breadth, lying about four miles west of, and several hundred feet above the Genesee River, thereby creating a vast water-power for so small a stream.

Some distance below the entrance of the outlet of Silver Lake into the river, is from twenty to twenty-five acres of alluvial flats in a perfect dell. It was purchased many years ago by a man who now re-sides on it, although his land extends over the high bank, and includes handsome level land there. It is certain that he and his family do go in and out of this dell, and that he gets in cattle and other domestic animals; but it would test the science of an engineer to ascertain how he effects it.

At the distance of eleven miles from St. Helena is Mount Morris,[6] on the right or eastern side of the river, and Squawkie Hill on the left or western. These are not mountains, or even hills, within the common acceptance of the words, hut merely a descent of two or three hundred feet, and that not abrupt, nor is its existence in any par-ticular line of demarcation observable, from the upper plateau of land through which the depressed channel of Genesee River runs down to Genesee Flats.

From Mount Morris and Squawkie Hill, where the river disputes itself from the thraldom of its rocky and precipitous hanks, it moves slowly, taking a serpentine course through the Genesee and other flats: the high grounds on each side gradually diminishing in height, and the alluvial flats decreasing in width in proportion, until the stream merely flows in its shallow channel through a Champaign country, before it reaches the great falls at Rochester, near forty miles from Mount Morris, where, after passing the rapids, it falls ninety-six feet perpendicularly into a chasm below, through which it flows one and a half miles further, and then passes two more perpendicular falls, within a short distance of each other, the upper one of twenty-five feet, and the lower of eighty-four feet. At the foot of these falls the river be-comes navigable for steamboats, and runs sluggishly live miles through a deep ravine a portion of the way to its mouth, where it disembogues

---

5. *Gä-ná-yät*—Its signification is lost.
6. The name of Mount Morris, in the Seneca dialect, was *So-nó-jo-wan-ga*. This was the name of Big Kettle, an orator not less distinguished among the Senecas than Red Jacket himself.

itself into Lake Ontario.

Bigtree[7] village, which bore the name of one of its chief? was a small village lying a mile and a half north of Little Beard's Town. Ten miles still further down the river was situated Cannewagus[8] village, a place of some note for a sub-village. This was the residence of the patriarch Hot Bread.

Tonawanda Indian village, whose inhabitants have always been remarkable for their peaceable and quiet disposition, is situated on the Tonawanda Creek, about forty miles north-west of Little Beard's Town, on the great Indian trail from east to west passing through this country. The Great Bend of the Tonawanda creek, between Little Beard's Town and the Tonawanda village, where the village of Batavia now stands, was a noted camping-ground for the Indians while passing to and fro on this trail. Still further north-west, thirty-two miles from Tonawanda village, is Tuscarora village, inhabited by the most civilized, agricultural, mechanical, and commercial tribe of the Six Nations. Lewiston is three miles west of Tuscarora village, and Fort Niagara is seven miles north of Lewiston, making the whole route from Little Beard's Town to Fort Niagara, following this trail, eighty-two miles.

From Lewiston seven miles south was Fort Schlosser, a mere stockade fort; the Devil's Hole being about midway between those two points. Fort Schlosser was at the northern termination of the navigable waters of the Niagara River above the falls; and this seven miles from Lewiston to Schlosser was the only place requiring land transportation for men, stores. or merchandise, from Quebec to Fort Mackinaw, or indeed, from the Atlantic Ocean to the end of Lake Superior. These forts, therefore, Niagara and Schlosser, were considered very important by the contending parties in olden times, the French and the English.

From Tonawanda village about twenty-five miles south-westerly lies the first Indian village on the Buffalo Creek, along which and its several branches there are a number of Indian villages and single *wig-*

7. The word *Gä-un-do-wä-na*, which was the name of this village, signifies a "big tree."

8. The Iroquois still retain their geographical names with great fidelity. As their proper names are descriptive, they still form a part of their language. Wherever an American village sprang up on one of their known localities, the name of the old village was immediately transferred to the new, and down to the present time the Iroquois still call them by their original names. Thus, *Gä-no-wan-ges*, signifying "Stinking Water." The name of this Indian village was transferred to Avon, by which it is still known among them.

*wams.* Up the shore of Lake Erie in a south-western direction, about thirty-five miles from Buffalo Creek, is the village of Cattaraugus, situated on the creek of the same name, two or three miles from its mouth, being about one hundred miles from Little Beard's Town, following this circuitous trail, which was the one always travelled by the Indians, unless an experienced runner took a shorter cut, at his own hazard, in a case of emergency.

East of Little Beard's Town are Conesus, Hemlock, Candice, Honeoye, Canandaigua, and Seneca Lakes; five miles west of the foot of the latter stood the famous Indian and Tory headquarters, called the "Old Castle." The foot of Canandaigua Lake is about ten miles west of the Old Castle, and thirty-four miles east of Little Beard's Town.

The Indian village of Can-ne-skrau-gah, meaning "among the slippery-elms," was situated about fourteen miles south-easterly of Mount Morris, on a creek of the same name, which empties into Genesee River near the latter place. This village stood on or near the ground now occupied by the village of Dansville. East of the junction of Genesee River and Canneskraugah Creek, extending some distance up the river and down the river, was a sparsely-settled Indian village or settlement, which appeared to be a kind of suburb of Genishau, or Little Beard's Town.[9]

Squawkie Hill village, lying about two miles south of Little Beard's Town, was a great resort for the Indians to enjoy their sportive games, gymnastic feats, and civic festivals.

Caneadea Indian village, or rather villages, were situated up the Genesee River on the Caneadea Flats, beginning at the mouth of Wiscoy, meaning "Many Fall," Creek, twenty miles from Mount Morris, and extending up the river, at intervals, eight or nine miles, nearly to the great angle in the river. From the southern end of Caneadea Indian settlement south-westerly about forty-five miles, on the Alleghany River, is the small Indian village called by Mrs. Jemison U-na-waum-gwa, but now known as Tu-ne-un-gwan. Further down the river is Kill Buck's Town, at the mouth of Great Valley Creek, and Buck Tooth's Town, at the mouth of Little Valley Creek. Below these is Che-na-shung-gan-tan or Te-ush-un-ush-un-gau-tau, being at the

---

9. *Da-yó-it-ga-o*, the name of this village, means "Where the river issues from the hills." It describes the place where the Genesee River emerges from between two narrow walls of rock, and enters the broad valley of the Genesee. This valley, separating itself from the river at this point, extends up to Dansville, and the Caneserauga Creek flows through it.

mouth of what is now called Cold Spring Creek, in the town of Napoli, Cattaraugus County, N. Y. This village is about eighteen miles below Tuneungwan. Below these are several Indian settlements along the river, the most considerable of which is Cornplanter's settlement, extending several miles along the river, Cornplanter himself being located near the centre.

Of the population of the several Indian villages and settlements at the time Mrs. Jemison emigrated to this section of country, we can make no estimate; and even in latter years, so wandering are the habits of the Indians that a village may be filled to overflowing, apparently, with residents, one month, and be almost depopulated the next. Their manner of lodging, cooking, and eating greatly facilitates their migratory propensities, as one large cabin will as well accommodate fifty as five. A deer-skin for a bed, a large kettle for a boiler, hot ashes or embers for an oven, a bark trough for a soup-dish and platter, a chip for a plate, a knife, (which each carries,) a sharp stick for a fork, and, perhaps, a wooden spoon and tin cup, comprehend a complete set' of household furniture, cooking and eating utensils. Even at this day, the only time the number of individuals who compose a tribe is known, or pretended to be known, is when they are about to receive their annuities; and it is then impossible to ascertain a " local habitation or a name" for but few of the individuals for whom annuities are drawn as belonging to such a tribe.

The following statement of the numbers and location of the Indians composing the Six Nations, in 1823, is a specimen of the precision adopted in the transaction of our public business relative to Indian affairs. This account was obtained from Captain Horatio Jones, who was the United States agent for paying the annuities to the Six Nations.

The individuals belonging to the Six Nations, in the state of New York, are located on their reservations from Oneida Lake westward to Lake Erie and Alleghany River, and amount to five thousand. Those located in Ohio on the Sandusky River amount to six hundred and eighty-eight, to wit: three hundred and eighty Cayugas, one hundred Senecas, sixty-four Mohawks, sixty-four Oneidas, and eighty Onondagas. The bulk of the Mohawks, together with some of each of the other five na tions, reside on the Grand River, in Upper Canada.

CHAPTER 6

# Death of She-nan-jee

When we arrived at Genishau, the Indians of that tribe were making active preparations for joining the French, in order to assist them in retaking Fort Ne-a-gaw[1] (as Fort Niagara was called in the Seneca language) from the British, who had taken it from the French in the month preceding. They marched off the next day after our arrival, painted and accoutred in all the *habiliments* of Indian warfare, determined on death or victory; and joined the army in season to assist in accomplishing a plan that had been previously concerted for the destruction of a part of the British army.

The British feeling themselves secure in the possession of Fort Neagaw, and unwilling that their enemies should occupy any of the military posts in that quarter, determined to take Fort Schlosser,— lying a few miles up the river from Neagaw,—which they expected to effect with but little loss. Accordingly a detachment of soldiers, sufficiently numerous, as was supposed, was sent out to take it, leaving a strong garrison in the fort, and marched off, well prepared to effect their object. But on their way they were surrounded by the French and Indians, who lay in ambush to deceive them, and were driven back with great loss. Our Indians were absent but a few days, and returned in triumph, bringing with them two white prisoners, and a number of oxen. Those were the first neat cattle that were ever brought to the Genesee flats.

The next day after their return to Genishau, was set apart as a day of feasting and frolicking, at the expense of the lives of their two

1. The Seneca name of the Niagara River, and of Lake Ontario, was Ne-ah-gä. They derived the name from a locality near the site of Youngstown, in the vicinity of which is the present Fort Niagara. Our present name Niagara, is derived from this word.

unfortunate prisoners, on whom they purposed to glut their revenge, and satisfy their love for retaliation upon their enemies. My sister was anxious to attend the execution, and to take me with her, to witness the customs of the warriors, as it was one of the highest kind of frolics ever celebrated in their tribe, and one that was not often attended with so much pomp and parade as it was expected that would be. I felt a kind of anxiety to witness the scene, having never attended an execution, and yet I felt a kind of horrid dread that made my heart revolt, and inclined me to step back rather than support the idea of advancing. On the morning of the execution she made her intention of going to the frolic, and taking me with her, known to our mother, who in the most feeling terms, remonstrated against a step at once so rash and unbecoming the true dignity of our sex:

"How, my daughter," (said she, addressing my sister,) "how can you even think of attending the feast and seeing the unspeakable torments that those poor unfortunate prisoners must inevitably suffer from the hands of our warriors? How can you stand and see them writhing in the warriors' fire, in all the agonies of a slow, a lingering death?

"How can you think of enduring the sound of their groanings and prayers to the Great Spirit for sudden deliverance from their enemies, or from life? And how can you think of conducting to that melancholy spot your poor sister Deh-he-wä-mis, (meaning myself), who has so lately been a prisoner, who has lost her parents and brothers by the hands of the bloody warriors, and who has felt all the horrors of the loss of her freedom, in lonesome captivity? Oh! how can you think of making her bleed at the wounds which now are but partially healed?

"The recollection of her former troubles would deprive us of Deh-he-wä-mis, and she would depart to the fields of the blessed, where fighting has ceased, and the corn needs no tending—where hunting is easy, the forests delightful, the summers are pleasant, and the winters are mild! O! think once, my daughter, how soon you may have a brave brother made prisoner in battle, and sacrificed to feast the ambition of the enemies of his kindred, and leave us to mourn for the loss of a friend, a son and a brother, whose bow brought us venison, and supplied us with blankets! Our task is quite easy at home, and our business needs our attention. With war we have nothing to do: our husbands and brothers are proud to defend us, and their hearts beat with ardour to meet our proud foes. Oh! stay then, my daughter; let our warriors alone perform on their victims their customs of war!"

This speech of our mother had the desired effect; we stayed at home and attended to our domestic concerns. The prisoners, however, were executed by having their heads taken off, their bodies cut in pieces and shockingly mangled, and then burnt to ashes! They were burnt on the north side of Fallbrook, directly opposite the town which was on the south side, sometime in the month of November, 1759.

Our Indians were also among those who lay in ambush on the Niagara River to intercept a party of the British who were guarding a quantity of baggage from Lewiston to Fort Schlosser. When the British party arrived at the designated point, the Indians arose from their ambush, and drove the British off the bank of the river, into a place called the Devil's Hole, together with their horses, carriages, and loading, and everything belonging to the party. Not a man escaped being driven off; and of the whole number, one only was fortunate enough to escape with life.[2]

I spent the winter comfortably, and as agreeably as I could have expected to, in the absence of my kind husband. Spring at length appeared, but Sheninjee was yet away; summer came on, but my husband had not found me. Fearful forebodings haunted my imagination; yet I felt confident that his affection for me was so great that if he was alive he would follow me and I should again see him. In the course of the summer, however, I received intelligence that soon after he left me at Yiskahwana he was taken sick and died at Wiishto. This was a heavy and an unexpected blow. I was now in my youthful days left a widow, with one son, and entirely dependent on myself for his and my support. My mother and her family gave me all the consolation in their power, and in a few months my grief wore off and I became contented.

In a year or two after this, according to my best recollection of the time, the King of England offered a bounty to those who would bring in the prisoners that had been taken in the war, to some military post where they might be redeemed and set at liberty.

John Van Sice, a Dutchman, who had frequently been at our place, and was well acquainted with every prisoner at Genishau, resolved to take me to Niagara, that I might there receive my liberty and he the offered bounty. I was notified of his intention; but as I was fully determined not to be redeemed at that time, especially with his assistance, I carefully watched his movements in order to avoid falling into his hands. It so happened, however, that he saw me alone at work

2. See Appendix, "Tragedy of Devil's Hole."

in a cornfield, and thinking probably that he could secure me easily, ran towards me in great haste. I espied him at some distance, and well knowing the amount of his errand, run from him with all the speed I was mistress of, and never once stopped till I reached Gardeau. He gave up the chase, and returned: but I, fearing that he might be lying in wait for me, stayed three days and three nights in an old cabin at Gardeau, and then went back trembling at every step for fear of being apprehended. I got home without difficulty; and soon after, the chiefs in council having learned the cause of my elopement, gave orders that I should not be taken to any military post without my consent; and that as it was my choice to stay, I should live amongst them quietly and undisturbed.

But, notwithstanding the will of the chiefs, it was but a few days before the old king of our tribe told one of my Indian brothers that I should be redeemed, and he would take me to Niagara himself. In reply to the old king,[3] my brother said that I should not be given up; but that, as it was my wish, I should stay with the tribe as long as I was pleased to. Upon this a serious quarrel ensued between them, in which my brother frankly told him that sooner than I should be taken by force, he would kill me with his own hands! Highly enraged at the old king; my brother came to my sister's house, where I resided, and informed her of all that had passed respecting me; and that, if the old king should attempt to take me, as he firmly believed he would, he would immediately take my life, and hazard the consequences. He returned to the old king.

As soon as I came in, my sister told me what she had just heard, and what she expected without doubt would befall me. Full of pity, and anxious for my preservation, she then directed me to take my

---

3. There is no propriety whatever in calling any of the Seneca chiefs by this title. The nation was originally governed by eight *sachems*, all of whom were equal in rank and authority; and the title was hereditary in the tribe, although not strictly in the family of the individual. The son could never succeed his father, because the father and son were always of different tribes. There were eight tribes in the Seneca nation—the Wolf, Bear, Beaver, Deer, Turtle, Snipe, Heron, and Hawk.
No man was allowed to marry into his own tribe; and the children were of the tribe of the mother. The title being hereditary in the tribe, the son was thereby excluded from the succession.
At a later day, a class of chiefs were created subordinate to the *sachems*; but in course of time they came to have an equal voice with the *sachems* in the administration of the affairs of the nation. The office was elective, and for life, and was not hereditary. To this day, (as at time of first publication), they have the eight *sachems*, still holding by the ancient tenure, and about seventy chiefs.

child and go into some high weeds at no great distance from the house, and there hide myself and lay still till all was silent in the house, for my brother, she said, would return at evening and let her know the final conclusion of the matter, of which she promised to inform me in the following manner: If I was to be killed, she said she would bake a small cake and lay it at the door, on the outside, in a place that she then pointed out to me. When all was silent in the house, I was to creep softly to the door, and if the cake could not be found in the place specified, I was to go in: but if the cake was there, I was to take my child and; go as fast as I possibly could to a large spring on the south side of Samp's Creek, (a place that I had often seen,) and there wait till I should by some means hear from her.

Alarmed for my own safety, I instantly followed her advice, and went into the weeds, where I lay in a state of the greatest anxiety, till all was silent in the house, when I crept to the door, and there found, to my great distress, the little cake! I knew my fate was fixed, unless I could keep secreted till the storm was over, and accordingly crept back to the weeds, where my little Thomas lay, took him on my back, and laid my course for the spring as fast as my legs would carry me. Thomas was nearly three years old, and very large and heavy. I got to the spring early in the morning, almost overcome with fatigue, and at the same time fearing that I might be pursued and taken, I felt my life an almost insupportable burthen. I sat down with my child at the spring, and he and I made a breakfast of the little cake, and water of the spring, which I dipped and supped with the only implement which I possessed,—my hand.

In the morning after I fled, as was expected, the old king came to our house in search of me, and to take me off; but, as I was not to be found, he gave me up, and went to Niagara with the prisoners he had already got into his possession.

As soon as the old king was fairly out of the way, my sister told my brother where he could find me. He immediately set out for the spring, and found me about noon. The first sight of him made me tremble with the fear of death; but when he came near,—so near that I could discover his countenance,—tears of joy flowed down my cheeks, and I felt such a kind of instant relief as no one can possibly experience, unless when under the absolute sentence of death he receives an unlimited pardon.

We were both rejoiced at the failure of the old king's project; and after staying at the spring through the night, set out together for home early in the morning. When we got to a cornfield near the town, my brother secreted me till he could go and ascertain how my case stood; and finding that the old king was absent, and that all was peaceable, he returned to me, and I went home joyfully.

Not long after this, my mother went to Johnstown, on the Mohawk River, with five prisoners, who were redeemed by Sir William Johnson, and set at liberty.

When my son Thomas was three or four years old, I was married to an Indian, whose name was Hiokatoo, commonly called Gardeau, by whom I had four daughters and two sons. I named my children, principally, after my relatives, from whom I was parted, by calling my girls Jane, Nancy, Betsey and Polly, and the boys John and Jesse. Jane died about twenty-nine years ago, in the month of August, a little before the great Council at Big-Tree, aged about fifteen years. My other daughters are yet living, and have families, (as at time of first publication).

# CHAPTER 7

# Treaty With the British

After the conclusion of the French war, our tribe had nothing to trouble it till the commencement of the Revolution. For twelve or fifteen years the use of the implements of war was not known, nor the war-whoop heard, save on days of festivity, when the achievements of former times were commemorated in a kind of mimic warfare, in which the chiefs and warriors displayed their prowess, and illustrated their former adroitness, by laying the ambuscade, surprising their enemies, and performing many accurate manoeuvres with the tomahawk and scalping knife; thereby preserving and handing to their children, the theory of Indian warfare. During that period they also pertinaciously observed the religious rites of their progenitors, by attending with the most scrupulous exactness and a great degree of enthusiasm to the sacrifices, at particular times, to appease the anger of the evil deity, or to excite the commiseration and friendship of the Great Good Spirit, whom they adored with reverence, as the author, governor, supporter and disposer of every good thing of which they participated.

They also practised in various athletic games, such as running, wrestling, leaping, and playing ball, with a view that their bodies might be more supple,—or rather that they might not become enervated, and that they might be enabled to make a proper selection of chiefs for the councils of the nation and leaders for war.

While the Indians were thus engaged in their round of traditionary performances, with the addition of hunting, their women attended to agriculture, their families, and a few domestic concerns of small consequence, and attended with but little labour.

No people can live more happy than the Indians did in times of peace, before the introduction of spirituous liquors amongst them.

In Indian costume at the age of sixteen

Their lives were a continual round of pleasures. Their wants were few, and easily satisfied; and their cares were only for today—the bounds of their calculations for future comfort not extending to the incalculable uncertainties of tomorrow. If peace ever dwelt with men, it was in former times, in the recesses from war, amongst what are now termed barbarians. The moral character of the Indians was (if I may be allowed the expression) uncontaminated. Their fidelity was perfect, and became proverbial; they were strictly honest; they despised deception and falsehood; and chastity was held in high veneration, and a violation of it was considered sacrilege. They were temperate in their desires, moderate in their passions, and candid and honourable in the expression of their sentiments on every subject of importance.

Thus, at peace amongst themselves, and with the neighbouring whites,—though there were none at that time very near,—our Indians lived quietly and peaceably at home, till a little before the breaking out of the revolutionary war, when they were sent for, together with the chiefs and members of the Six Nations generally, by the people of the States, to go to the German Flats, and there hold a general council, in order that the people of the states might ascertain, in good season, who they should esteem and treat as enemies, and who as friends, in the great war which was then upon the point of breaking out between them and the King of England.

Our Indians obeyed the call, and the council was holden, at which the pipe of peace was smoked, and a treaty made, in which the Six Nations solemnly agreed that if a war should eventually break out, they would not take up arms on either side; but that they would observe a strict neutrality. With that the people of the states were satisfied, as they had not asked their assistance, nor did not wish it. The Indians returned to their homes well pleased that they could live on neutral ground, surrounded by the din of war, without being engaged in it.

About a year passed off, and we, as usual, were enjoying ourselves in the employments of peaceable times, when a messenger arrived from the British commissioners, requesting all the Indians of our tribe to attend a general council which was soon to be held at Oswego. The council convened, and being opened, the British commissioners informed the chiefs that the object of calling a council of the Six Nations, was, to engage their assistance in subduing the rebels—the people of the states, who had risen up against the good king, their master, and were about to rob him of a great part of his possessions and wealth—and added that they would amply reward them for all their services.

The chiefs then arose, and informed the commissioners of the nature and extent of the treaty which they had entered into with the people of the states, the year before, and that they should not violate it by taking up the hatchet against them.

The commissioners continued their entreaties without success, till they addressed their avarice, by telling our people that the people of the states were few in number, and easily subdued; and that on the account of their disobedience to the king, they justly merited all the punishment that it was possible for white men and Indians to inflict upon them; and added, that the king was rich and powerful, both in money and subjects: That his rum was as plenty as the water in Lake Ontario: that his men were as numerous as the sands upon the lake shore; and that the Indians, if they would assist in the war, and persevere in their friendship to the king, till it was closed, should never want for money or goods. Upon this the chiefs concluded a treaty with the British commissioners, in which they agreed to take up arms against the rebels, and continue in the service of His Majesty till they were subdued, in consideration of certain conditions which were stipulated in the treaty to be performed by the British government and its agents.[1]

As soon as the treaty was finished, the commissioners made a present to each Indian of a suit of clothes, a brass kettle, a gun and tomahawk, a scalping knife, a quantity of powder and lead a piece of gold, and promised a bounty on every scalp that should be brought in. Thus richly clad and equipped, they returned home, after an absence of about two weeks, full of the fire of war, and anxious to encounter their enemies. Many of the kettles which the Indians received at that time are now in use on the Genesee Flats.

Hired to commit depredations upon the whites, who had given them no offence, they waited impatiently to commence their labour, till sometime in the spring of 1776, when a convenient opportunity offered for them to make an attack. At that time, a party of our Indians were at Cau-te-ga, who shot a man that was looking after his horse, for the sole purpose, as I was informed by my Indian brother, who

---

1. Unanimity was a fundamental law of the Iroquois civil polity. When the question of joining the English came before the council of the League, the Oneidas refused to concur, and thus defeated the measure ; but it was agreed that each nation might engage in it upon its own responsibility. It was impossible to keep the Mohawks from the English alliance.

was present, of commencing hostilities. In May following, our Indians were in their first battle with the Americans; but at what place I am unable to determine. While they were absent at that time, my daughter Nancy was born.

The same year, at Cherry Valley, our Indians took a woman and her three daughters prisoners, and brought them on, leaving one at Canandaigua, one at Honeoye, one at Cattaraugus, and one (the woman) at Little Beard's Town, where I resided. The woman told me that she and her daughters might have escaped, but that they expected the British army only, and therefore made no effort. Her husband and sons got away. After some time, they were all taken to Fort Niagara, where they were redeemed by Colonel Butler, well clothed, and sent home—except one daughter, who was married to a British officer at the fort, by the name of Johnson. Johnson was of the party who captured her; at which time he very unceremoniously took from her finger a gold ring, and appropriated it to his own use. When he saw her again at Niagara he recognized her, restored the ring that he had so impolitely borrowed, courted and married her; and although the marriage ceremony was celebrated in a wilderness, far from the rendezvous of civilized society, and destitute of the facilities of obtaining the elegances, conveniences, or even the necessaries of life, they were singularly provided with a wedding-ring.

In the same expedition, Joseph Smith was taken prisoner at or near Cherry Valley, brought to Genesee, and detained till after the Revolutionary War. He was then liberated, and the Indians made him a present, in company with Horatio Jones, of 6000 acres of land lying in the present town of Leicester, in the county of Livingston.

Previous to the battle at Fort Stanwix, the British sent for the Indians to come and see them whip the rebels; and, at the same time stated that they did not wish to have them fight, but wanted to have them just sit down smoke their pipes, and look on. Our Indians went, to a man; but contrary to their expectation, instead of smoking and looking on, they were obliged to fight for their lives, and in the end of the battle were completely beaten, with a great loss in killed and wounded. Our Indians alone had thirty-six killed, and a great number wounded. Our town exhibited a scene of real sorrow and distress, when our warriors returned and recounted their misfortunes, and stated the real loss they had sustained in the engagement. The mourning was excessive, and was expressed by the most doleful yells, shrieks, and howlings, and by inimitable gesticulations.

During the revolution, my house was the home of Colonels Butler and Brandt, whenever they chanced to come into our neighbourhood as they passed to and from Fort Niagara, which was the seat of their military operations. Many and many a night I have pounded *samp* for them from sunset till sunrise, and furnished them with necessary provision and clean clothing for their journey.

CHAPTER 8

# Approach of General Sullivan's Army

For four or five years we sustained no loss in the war, except in the few who had been killed in distant battles; and our tribe, because of the remoteness of its situation, from the enemy, felt secure from an attack. At length, in the fall of 1779, intelligence was received that a large and powerful army of the rebels, under the command of General Sullivan, was making rapid progress towards our settlement, burning and destroying the huts and cornfields; killing the cattle, hogs and horses, and cutting down the fruit trees belonging to the Indians throughout the country.[1]

Our Indians immediately became alarmed, and suffered everything but death from fear that they should be taken by surprise, and totally destroyed at a single blow. But in order to prevent so great a catastrophe, they sent out a few spies who were to keep themselves at a short distance in front of the invading army, in order to watch its operations, and give information of its advances and success.

Sullivan arrived at Canandaigua Lake, and had finished his work of destruction there, and it was ascertained that he was about to march to our flats, when our Indians resolved to give him battle on the way, and prevent, if possible, the distresses to which they knew we should be subjected, if he should succeed in reaching our town. Accordingly they sent all their women and children into the woods a little west of Little Beard's Town, in order that we might make a good retreat if it should be necessary, and then, well armed, set out to face the conquering enemy. The place which they fixed upon for their battle ground lay between Honeoye Creek and the head of Conesus Lake.

At length a scouting party from Sullivan's army arrived at the spot

---

1. See Appendix—"General Sullivan's Expedition."

selected, when the Indians arose from their ambush with all the fierceness and terror that it was possible for them to exercise, and directly put the party upon a retreat. Two Oneida Indians were all the prisoners that were taken in that skirmish. One of them was a pilot of General Sullivan, and had been very active in the war, rendering to the people of the states essential services. At the commencement of the revolution he had a brother older than himself, who resolved to join the British service, and endeavoured by all the art that he was capable of using to persuade his brother to accompany him; but his arguments proved abortive. This went to the British, and that joined the American army. At this critical juncture they met, one in the capacity of a conqueror, the other in that of a prisoner; and as an Indian seldom forgets a countenance that he has seen, they recognized each other at sight. Envy and revenge glared in the features of the conquering savage, as he advanced to his brother (the prisoner) in all the haughtiness of Indian pride, heightened by a sense of power, and addressed him in the following manner:

"Brother, you have merited death! The hatchet or the war-club shall finish your career! When I begged of you to follow me in the fortunes of war, you was deaf to my cries—you spurned my entreaties!

"Brother! you have merited death and shall have your deserts! When the rebels raised their hatchets to fight their good master, you sharpened your knife, you brightened your rifle and led on our foes to the fields of our fathers! You have merited death and shall die by our hands! When those rebels had drove us from the fields of our fathers to seek out new homes, it was you who could dare to step forth as their pilot, and conduct them even to the doors of our *wigwams*, to butcher our children and put us to death! No crime can be greater! But though you have merited death and shall die on this spot, my hands shall not be stained in the blood of a brother! *Who will strike?*"

Little Beard, who was standing by, as soon as the speech was ended, struck the prisoner on the head with his tomahawk, and despatched him at once!

Little Beard then informed the other Indian prisoner that as they were at war with the whites only, and not with the Indians, they would spare his life, and after a while give him his liberty in an honourable manner. The Oneida warrior, however, was jealous of Little Beard's fidelity; and suspecting that he should soon fall by his hands, watched for a favourable opportunity to make his escape; which he soon effected. Two Indians were leading him, one on each side, when he made a violent effort, threw them upon the ground, and run for his life towards where the main body of the American army was encamped. The Indians pursued him without success; but in their absence they fell in with a small detachment of Sullivan's men, with whom they had a short but severe skirmish, in which they killed a number of the enemy, took Captain (or Lieutenant) William Boyd and one private, prisoners, and brought them to Little Beard's Town, where they were soon after put to death in the most shocking and cruel manner. Little Beard, in this, as in all other scenes of cruelty that happened at his town, was master of ceremonies, and principal actor.

Poor Boyd was stripped of his clothing, and then tied to a sapling, where the Indians menaced his life by throwing their tomahawks at the tree, directly over his head, brandishing their scalping knives around him in the most frightful manner, and accompanying their ceremonies with terrific shouts of joy. Having punished him sufficiently in this way, they made a small opening in his abdomen, took out an intestine, which they tied to the sapling, and then unbound him from the tree, and drove him round it till he had drawn out the whole of his intestines. He was then beheaded, his head was stuck upon a pole, and his body left on the ground unburied.

Thus ended the life of poor William Boyd, who, it was said, had every appearance of being an active and enterprising officer, of the first talents.[2] The other prisoner was (if I remember distinctly) only beheaded and left near Boyd.

This tragedy being finished, our Indians again held a short council on the expediency of giving Sullivan battle, if he should continue to advance, and finally came to the conclusion that they were not strong enough to drive him, nor to prevent his taking possession of their fields: but that if it was possible they would escape with their own lives, preserve their families, and leave their possessions to be overrun by the invading army.

The women and children were then sent on still further towards Buffalo, to a large creek that was called by the Indians Catawba, (Stony Creek, which empties into the Tonawanda Creek at Varysburg, Wyoming County), accompanied by a part of the Indians, while the remainder secreted themselves in the woods back of Little Beard's Town, to watch the movements of the army.

At that time I had three children who went with me on foot, one

2. See Appendix—"Removal of the remains of Lieutenant Boyd."

who rode on horseback, and one whom I carried on my back.

Our corn was good that year; a part of which we had gathered and secured for winter.

In one or two days after the skirmish at Conesus Lake, Sullivan and his army arrived at Genesee River, where they destroyed every article of the food kind that they could lay their hands on. A pan of our corn they burnt, and threw the remainder into the river. They burnt our houses, killed what few cattle and horses they could find, destroyed our fruit trees, and left nothing but the bare soil and timber. But the Indians had eloped and were not to be found.

Having crossed and recrossed the river, and finished the work of destruction, the army marched off to the east. Our Indians saw them move off, but suspecting that it was Sullivan's intention to watch our return, and then to take us by surprise, resolved that the main body of our tribe should hunt where *we* then were, till Sullivan had gone so far that there would be no danger of his returning to molest us.

This being agreed to, we hunted continually till the Indians concluded that there could be no risk in our once more taking possession of our lands. Accordingly we all returned; but what were our feelings when we found that there was not a mouthful of any kind of sustenance left—not even enough to keep a child one day from perishing with hunger.

The weather by this time had become cold and stormy; and as we were destitute of houses and food too, I immediately resolved to take my children and look out for myself, without delay. With this intention I took two of my little ones on my back, bade the other three follow, and the same night arrived on the Gardeau flats, where I have ever since resided, (as at time of first publication).

At that time, two negroes, who had run away from their masters sometime before, were the only inhabitants of those flats. They lived in a small cabin and had planted and raised a large field of corn, which they had not yet harvested. As they were in want of help to secure their crop, I hired to them to husk corn till the whole was harvested.

I have laughed a thousand times to myself when I have thought of the good old negro, who hired me, who fearing that I should get taken or injured by the Indians, stood by me constantly when I was husking, with a loaded gun in his hand, in order to keep off the enemy, and thereby lost as much labour of his own as he received from me, by paying good wages. I, however, was not displeased with his attention; for I knew that I should need all the corn that I could earn, even if I should husk the whole. I husked enough for them, to gain for myself, at every tenth string, one hundred strings of ears, which were equal to twenty-five bushels of shelled corn. This seasonable supply made my family comfortable for *samp* and cakes through the succeeding winter, which was the most severe that I have witnessed since my remembrance.

The snow fell about five feet deep, and remained so for a long time, and the weather was extremely cold; so much so indeed, that almost all the game upon which the Indians depended for subsistence, perished, and reduced them almost to a state of starvation through that and three or four succeeding years. When the snow melted in the spring, deer were found dead upon the ground in vast numbers; and other animals, of every description, perished from the cold also, and were found dead, in multitudes. Many of our people barely escaped with their lives, and some actually died of hunger and freezing.

But to return from this digression: Having been completely routed at Little Beard's Town, deprived of a house, and without the means of building one in season, after I had finished my husking, and having found from the short acquaintance which I had had with the negroes, that they were kind and friendly, I concluded, at their request, to take up my residence with them for a while in their cabin, till I should be able to provide a hut for myself. I lived more comfortable than I expected to through the winter, and the next season made a shelter for myself.

The negroes continued on my flats two or three years after this, and then left them for a place that they expected would suit them much better. But as that land became my own in a few years, by virtue of a deed from the Chiefs of the Six Nations, I have lived there from that to the present time, (as at time of first publication).

My flats were cleared before I saw them; and it was the opinion of the oldest Indians that were at Genishau, at the time that I first went there, that all the flats on the Genesee River were improved before any of the Indian tribes ever saw them.

I well remember that soon after I went to Little Beard's Town, the banks of Fall-Brook were washed off, which left a large number of human bones uncovered. The Indians then said that those were not the bones of Indians, because they had never heard of any of their dead being buried there; but that they were the bones of a race of men who a great many moons before, cleared that land and lived on the flats.

The next summer after Sullivan's campaign,[3] our Indians, highly incensed at the whites for the treatment they had received, and the sufferings which they had consequently endured, determined to obtain some redress by destroying their frontier settlements. Corn Planter, otherwise called John O'Bail, led the Indians, and an officer by the name of Johnston commanded the British in the expedition. The force was large, and so strongly bent upon revenge and vengeance, that seemingly nothing could avert its march, nor prevent its depredations. After leaving Genesee they marched directly to some of the head waters of the Susquehannah River, and Schoharie Creek, went down that creek to the Mohawk River, thence up that river to Fort Stanwix, and from thence came home. In their route they burnt a number of places; destroyed all the cattle and other property that fell in their way; killed a number of white people, and brought home a few prisoners.

In that expedition, when they came to Fort Plain, on the Mohawk River, Cornplanter and a party of his Indians took old John O'Bail, a white man, and made him a prisoner. Old John O'Bail, in his younger days had frequently passed through the Indian settlements that lay between the Hudson and Fort Niagara, and in some of his excursions had become enamoured with a squaw, by whom he had a son that was called Cornplanter.

Cornplanter,[4] was a chief of considerable eminence; and having been informed of his parentage and of the place of his father's residence, took the old man at this time, in order that he might make an introduction leisurely, and become acquainted with a man to whom, though a stranger, he was satisfied that he owed his existence.

After he had taken the old man, his father, he led him as a prisoner ten or twelve miles up the river, and then stepped before him, faced about, and addressed him in the following terms:—

My name is John O'Bail, commonly called Cornplanter. I am your son! you are my father! You are now my prisoner, and subject to the customs of Indian warfare: but you shall not be harmed—you need not fear. I am a warrior! Many are the scalps which I have taken! Many prisoners I have tortured to death! I am your son! I am a warrior! I was anxious to see you, and to greet you in friendship! I went to your cabin and took you by force! But your life shall be spared. Indians love their

3. *Narratives of Sullivan's Expedition, 1779* by John L. Hardenbergh, William McKendry, William Elliott Griffis & Simon L. Adler, also published by Leonaur.
4. Cornplanter's tomahawk is now in the State Indian Collection at Albany.

friends and their kindred, and treat them with kindness. If now you choose to follow the fortune of your yellow son, and to live with our people, I will cherish your old age with plenty of venison, and you shall live easy: But if it is your choice to return to your fields and live with your white children, I will send a party of my trusty young men to conduct you back in safety. I respect you, my father; you have been friendly to Indians, and they are your friends.

Old John chose to return. Cornplanter, as good as his word, ordered an escort to attend him home, which they did with the greatest care.

Amongst the prisoners that were brought to Genesee, was William Newkirk, a man by the name of Price, and two negroes.

Price lived a while with Little Beard, and afterwards with Jack Berry, an Indian. When he left Jack Berry he went to Niagara, where he now resides, (as at time of first publication).

Newkirk was brought to Beard's Town, and lived with Little Beard and at Fort Niagara about one year, and then enlisted under Butler, and went with him on an expedition to the Monongahela.

About this time, one Ebenezer Allen ran away from Pennsylvania, and came to live among us. He was much at my house with my son Thomas; he was always honourable, kind, and even generous to me; but the history of his life is a tissue of crimes and baseness of the blackest dye. I have often heard him relate his inglorious feats, and confess crimes, the rehearsal of which made my blood curdle, as much accustomed as I was to hear of bloody and barbarous deeds.

# CHAPTER 9

# Mary is Offered Her Freedom

Soon after the close of the Revolutionary War, my Indian brother, Kau-jises-tau-ge-au, (which being interpreted signifies Black Coals,) offered me my liberty, and told me that if it was my choice I might go to my friends.

My son Thomas was anxious that I should go; and offered to go with me, and assist me on the journey, by taking care of the younger children, and providing food as we travelled through the wilderness. But the chiefs of our tribe, suspecting, from his appearance, actions, and a few warlike exploits, that Thomas would be a great warrior, or a good counsellor, refused to let him leave them on any account whatever.

To go myself, and leave him, was more than I felt able to do; for he had been kind to me, and was one on whom I placed great dependence. The chiefs refusing to let him go was one reason for my resolving to stay; but another, more powerful if possible, was, that I had got a large family of Indian children that I must take with me; and that, if I should be so fortunate as to find my relatives, they would despise them, if not myself, and treat us as enemies, or, at least, with a degree of cold indifference, which I thought I could not endure.

Accordingly, after I had duly considered the matter, I told my brother that it was my choice to stay and spend the remainder of my days with my Indian friends, and live with my family as I hitherto had done. He appeared well pleased with my resolution, and informed me that, as that was my choice, I should have a piece of land that I could call my own, where I could live unmolested, and have something at my decease to leave for the benefit of my children.

In a short time, he made himself ready to go to Upper Canada; but before he left us he told me he would speak to some of the chiefs at

75

Buffalo, to attend the great council, which he expected would convene in a few years at furthest and convey to me such a tract of land as I should select. My brother left us as he had proposed, and soon after died at Grand River.

Kaujisestaugeau was an excellent man, and ever treated me with kindness. Perhaps no one of his tribe, at any time, exceeded him in natural mildness of temper and warmth and tenderness of affection. If he had taken my life at the time when the avarice of the old king inclined him to procure my emancipation, it would have been done with a pure heart, and from good motives. He loved his friends, and was generally beloved. During the time that I lived in the family with him, he never offered the most trifling abuse; on the contrary, his whole conduct toward me was strictly honourable. I mourned his loss as that of a tender brother, and shall recollect him through life with emotions of friendship and gratitude.

I lived undisturbed, without hearing a word on the subject of my land, till the great council was held at Big Tree, in 1797, when Farmer's Brother, whose Indian name is Ho-na-ye-wus, sent for me to attend the council. When I got there, he told me that my brother had spoken to him to see that I had a piece of land reserved for my use; and that then was the time for me to receive it. He requested that I would choose for myself, and describe the bounds of a piece that would suit me. I accordingly told him the place of beginning, and then went round a tract that I judged would be sufficient for my purpose, (knowing that it would include the Gardeau Flats,) by stating certain bounds with which I was acquainted.

When the council was opened, and the business afforded a proper opportunity, Farmer's Brother presented my claim, and rehearsed the request of my brother. Red Jacket, whose Indian name is Sagu-yu-what-hah, (which, interpreted, is Keeper-awake,) opposed me and my claim with all his influence and eloquence. Farmer's Brother insisted upon the necessity, propriety, and expediency of his proposition, and got the land granted. The deed was made and signed, securing to me the title of all the land I had described; under the same restrictions and regulations that other Indian lands are subject to.

This tract is more than six miles long from east to west, and nearly four and three-fourths miles wide from north to south, containing seventeen thousand nine hundred and twenty-seven acres, with the Genesee River running centrally through it, from south to north. It has been known ever since as the Gardeau Tract, or the Gardeau Reservation.

Red Jacket not only opposed my claim at the council, but he withheld my money two or three years, on the account of my lands having been granted without his consent. Jasper Parrish and Horatio Jones, who had both been taken prisoners by the Indians, adopted and detained with them many years, the first being the Indian agent for the United States, and the other interpreter, interfered, and at length convinced Red Jacket that it was the white people, and not the Indians, who had given me the land; and compelled him to pay over all the money which he had retained on my account. My land derived its name, Gardeau, from a hill that is within its limits, which is called, in the Seneca language, Kautam. Kautam, when interpreted, signifies up and down, or down and up, and is applied to a hill that you ascend and descend in passing; or to a valley. It has been said that Gardeau was the name of my husband Hiokatoo, and that my land derived its name from him; that, however, is a mistake; for the old man always considered Gardeau a nickname, and was uniformly offended when called by it.

My flats were extremely fertile, but needed more labour than my daughters and myself were able to perform, to produce a sufficient quantity of grain and other necessary productions of the earth for the consumption of our family. The land had lain uncultivated so long that it was thickly covered with weeds of almost every description. In order that we might live more easy, Mr. Parrish, with the consent of the chiefs, gave me liberty to lease or let my land to white people to till on shares. I accordingly let out the greater part of my improvements, and have continued to do so, which makes my task less burdensome, while at the same time I am more comfortably supplied with the means of support.

About three hundred acres of my land, when I first saw it, was open flats, lying on the Genesee River, which is supposed was cleared by a race of inhabitants who preceded the first Indian settlements in this part of the country. The Indians are confident that many parts of this country were settled, and for a number of years occupied, by the people of whom their fathers never had any tradition, as they never had seen them. Whence those people originated, and whither they went, I have never heard one of the oldest and wisest Indians pretend to guess. When I first came to Genishau, the bank of Fall Brook had just slid off, and exposed a large number of human bones, which the Indians said were buried there long before their fathers ever saw the place, and that they did not know what kind of people they were. It, however, was, and is, believed by our people that they were not Indians.

The tradition of the Seneca Indians, in regard to their origin, is, that they broke out of the earth from a large mountain at the head of Canandaigua Lake; and that mountain they still venerate as the place of their birth. Thence they derive their name, "Ge-nun-de-wah,"[1] or "Great Hill," and are called "The Great Hill People," which is the true definition of the word Seneca.

The great hill at the head of Canandaigua Lake, from whence they sprung, is called Genundewah, and has for a long time past been the place where the Indians of that nation have met in council, to hold great talks, and to offer up prayers to the Great Spirit, on account of its having been their birthplace; and, also, in consequence of the destruction of a serpent at that place in ancient time, in a most miraculous manner, which threatened the destruction of the whole of the Senecas, and barely spared enough to commence replenishing the earth.

The Indians say, that the fort on the big hill, or Genundewah, near the head of Canandaigua Lake, was surrounded by a monstrous serpent, whose head and tail came together at the gate. A long time it lay there, confounding the people with its breath. At length they attempted to make their escape, some with their hominy blocks, and others with different implements of household furniture; and in marching out of the fort walked down the throat of the serpent. Two orphan children, who had escaped this general destruction by being left on this side of the fort, were informed, by an oracle, of the means by which they could get rid of their formidable enemy—which was, to take a small bow and a poisoned arrow, made of a kind of willow, and with that shoot the serpent under its scales.

This they did, and the arrow proved effectual; for, on its penetrating the skin, the serpent became sick, and, extending itself, rolled down the hill, destroying all the timber that was in its way, disgorging itself, and breaking wind greatly as it went. At every motion a human head was discharged, and rolled down the hill into the lake, where they lie at this day in a petrified state, having the hardness and appearance of stones; and the Pagan Indians of the Senecas believe, that all the little snakes were made of the blood of the great serpent, after it rolled into the lake.

To this day, (as at time of first publication), the Indians visit that

1. The true name of the Senecas is *Nun-da-wä-o-no*, from Nun-da-wä-o, "a great hill." Hence the name of Nunda from *Nun-dä-o*, "hilly."

sacred place to mourn the loss of their friends, and to celebrate some rites that are peculiar to themselves. To the knowledge of white people, there has been no timber on the great hill since it was first discovered by them, though it lay apparently in a state of nature for a great number of years, without cultivation. Stones in the shape of Indians' heads may be seen lying in the lake in great plenty, which are said to be the same that were deposited there at the death of the serpent.

The Senecas have a tradition, that previous to, and for some time after their origin at Genundewah, the country, especially about the lakes, was thickly inhabited by a race of civil, enterprising, and industrious people, who were totally destroyed by the great serpent that afterward surrounded the great hill fort, with the assistance of others of the same species; and that they (the Senecas) went into possession of the improvements that were left.

In those days the Indians throughout the whole country, as the Senecas say, spoke one language; but having become considerably numerous, the before-mentioned great serpent, by an unknown influence, confounded their language, so that they could not understand each other; which was the cause of their division into nations as the Mohawks, Oneidas, etc. At that time, however, the Senecas retained the original language, and continued to occupy their mother hill, on which they fortified themselves against their enemies, and lived peaceably, until having offended the serpent, they were cut off as I have before remarked.

CHAPTER 10

# Death of Hi-ok-a-too

From the time I secured my land, my life passed for many years
in an unvaried routine of superintending my family and taking care
of my property, without the occurrence of any event relative to me
or my affairs worth noticing, and but few in which the nation or our
villages felt much interest.

About the first of June, 1806, Little Beard died, and was buried
after the manner of burying chiefs. In his lifetime he had been quite
arbitrary, and had made some enemies whom he hated, probably, and
was not loved by them. The grave, however, deprives enmity of its
malignity, and revenge of its keenness.

Little Beard had been dead but a few days when the great eclipse
of the sun took place, on the 16th of June, which excited in the Indians a great degree of astonishment; for as they were ignorant of
astronomy, they were totally unqualified to account for so extraordi-
nary a phenomenon. The crisis was alarming, and something effectual
must be done without delay, to remove, if possible, such coldness and
darkness, which it was expected would increase. They accordingly ran
together in the three towns near the Genesee River, and after a long
consultation agreed that Little Beard, on the account of some old
grudge which he yet cherished toward them, had placed himself between them and the sun, in order that their corn might not grow, and
so reduce them to a state of starvation. Having thus found the cause,
the next thing was to remove it, which could only be done by the use
of powder and ball. Upon this, every gun and rifle was loaded, and a
firing commenced, that continued without cessation till the old fellow
left his seat, and the obscurity was entirely removed, to the great joy of
the ingenious and fortunate Indians.

I have frequently heard it asserted by white people, and can truly

80

say from my own experience, that the time at which parents take most satisfaction and comfort with their families, is when their children are young, incapable of providing for their own wants, and are about the fireside, where they can be duly observed and instructed.

In the government of their families among the Indians, the parents are very mild, the women superintending the children. The word of the father, however, is law, and must be obeyed by the whole who are under his authority.

The Indians are very tenacious of their precedence and supremacy over their wives, and the wives acknowledge it by their actions, with the greatest subserviency. It is a rule inculcated in all the Indian tribes, and practiced generation after generation, that a squaw shall not walk before her husband, or take the lead in *his* business. For this reason we never see a party on the march, in which squaws are not directly in the rear of their partners.

Few mothers, perhaps, have had less trouble with their children during their minority than myself. In general, my children were friendly to each other, and it was very seldom that I knew them to have the least difference or quarrel; so far indeed were they from rendering themselves or me uncomfortable, that I considered myself happy—more so than commonly falls to the lot of parents, especially to women.

My happiness in this respect, however, was not without alloy; for my son Thomas, from some cause unknown to me, from the time he was a small lad, always called his brother John a witch, which was the cause, as they grew toward manhood, of frequent and severe quarrels between them, and gave me much trouble and anxiety for their safety. After Thomas and John had arrived to the age of manhood, another source of contention arose between them, founded on the circumstance of John's having two wives. Although polygamy[1] was tolerated in our tribe, Thomas considered it a violation of good and wholesome rules in society, and tending directly to destroy that friendly social intercourse and love which ought to be the happy result of matrimony and chastity.

Consequently, he frequently reprimanded John, by telling him that his conduct was beneath the dignity, and inconsistent with the principles of good Indians; indecent, and unbecoming a gentleman; and, as he never could reconcile himself to it, he was frequently—almost

---

1. Although polygamy has prevailed to a limited extent among the Senecas in later times, it was prohibited in earlier days, and considered disgraceful.

constantly, when they were together—talking to him on the subject. John always resented such reprimand and reproof with a great degree of passion, though they never quarrelled, unless Thomas was intoxicated.

In his fits of drunkenness, Thomas seemed to lose all his natural reason, and to conduct like a wild or crazy man, without regard to relatives, decency, or propriety. At such times he often threatened to take my life for having raised a witch, (as he called John,) and has gone so far as to raise his tomahawk to split my head. He, however, never struck me; but on John's account he struck Hiokatoo, and thereby excited in John a high degree of indignation, which was extinguished only by blood.

For a number of years their difficulties and consequent unhappiness continued, and rather increased, continually exciting in my breast the most fearful apprehensions, and greatest anxiety for their safety. With tears in my eyes I advised them to become reconciled to each other, and to be friendly; told them the consequences of their continuing to cherish so much malignity and malice—that it would end in their destruction, the disgrace of their families, and bring me down to the grave. No one can conceive of the constant trouble that I daily endured on their account—on the account of my two oldest sons, whom I loved equally, and with all the feelings and affection of a tender mother, stimulated by an anxious concern for their fate.

Parents, mothers especially, will love their children, though ever so unkind and disobedient. Their eyes of compassion, of real sentimental affection, will be involuntarily extended after them, in their greatest excesses of iniquity; and those fine filaments of consanguinity, which gently entwine themselves around the heart where filial love and parental care are equal, will be lengthened and enlarged to cords seemingly of sufficient strength to reach and reclaim the wanderer. I know that such exercises are frequently unavailing; but notwithstanding their ultimate failure, it still remains true, and ever will, that the love of a parent for a disobedient child will increase, and grow more and more ardent, so long as a hope of its reformation is capable of stimulating a disappointed breast.

My advice and expostulations with my sons were abortive; and year after year their disaffection for each other increased. At length, Thomas came to my house on the first day of July, 1811, in my absence, somewhat intoxicated, where he found John, with whom he immediately commenced a quarrel on their old subjects of difference.

John's anger became desperate. He caught Thomas by the hair of his head, and dragged him out of the door, and there killed him, by a blow which he gave him on the head with his tomahawk.

I returned soon after, and found my son lifeless at the door, on the spot where he was killed. No one can judge of my feelings on seeing this mournful spectacle; and what greatly added to my distress was the fact that he had fallen by the murderous hand of his brother. I felt my situation insupportable. Having passed through various scenes of trouble of the most cruel and trying kind, I had hoped to spend my few remaining days in quietude, and to die in peace, surrounded by my family. This fatal event, however, seemed to be a stream of woe poured into my cup of afflictions, filling it even to overflowing, and blasting all my prospects.

As soon as I had recovered a little from the shock which I felt at the sight of my departed son, and some of the neighbours had come in to help take care of the corpse, I hired Shanks, an Indian, to go to Buffalo, and carry the sorrowful news of Thomas' death to our friends at that place, and request the chiefs to hold a council, and dispose of John as they should think proper. Shanks set out on his errand immediately, and John, fearing that he should be apprehended and punished for the crime he had committed, at the same time went off toward Caneadea.

Thomas was decently interred in a style corresponding with his rank.

The chiefs soon assembled in council on the trial of .John, and after having seriously examined the matter according to their laws, justified his conduct, and acquitted him. They considered Thomas to have been the first transgressor; and that, for the abuses which he had offered, he had merited from John the treatment that he had received. John, on learning the decision of the council, returned to his family.

Thomas, except when intoxicated, which was not frequent, was a kind and tender child, willing to assist me in my labour, and to remove every obstacle to my comfort. His natural abilities were said to be of a superior cast, and he soared above the trifling subjects of revenue which are common among Indians, as being far beneath his attention. In his childish and boyish days, his natural turn was to practice in the art of war, though he despised the cruelties that the warriors inflicted upon their subjugated enemies. He was manly in his deportment, courageous, and active; and commanded respect. Though he appeared well pleased with peace, he was cunning in Indian warfare, and succeeded to admiration in the execution of his plans.

At the age of fourteen or fifteen years, he went into the war with manly fortitude, armed with a tomahawk and scalping-knife; and, when he returned, brought one white man a prisoner, whom he had taken with his own hands, on the west branch of the Susquehanna River. It so happened, that as he was looking out for his enemies, he discovered two men boiling sap in the woods. He watched them unperceived till dark, when he advanced with a noiseless step to the place where they were standing, caught one of them before they were apprised of danger, and conducted him to the camp. He was well treated while a prisoner, and redeemed at the close of the war.

At the time Kaujisestaugeau gave me liberty to go to my friends, Thomas was anxious to go with me; but as I have before observed, the chiefs would not suffer him to leave them, on the account of his courage and skill in war: expecting that they should need his assistance. He was a great counsellor, and a chief when quite young; and, in the last capacity, went two or three times to Philadelphia, to assist in making treaties with the people of the states.

Thomas, at the time of his death, was a few moons over fifty-two years old. He was then living with his fourth wife, having lost three; by whom he had eight children. As he was naturally good-natured, and possessed a friendly disposition, he would not have come to so untimely a death, had it not been for his intemperance. He fell a victim to the use of ardent spirits: a poison that will soon exterminate the Indian tribes in this part of the country, and leave their names without root or branch. The thought is melancholy; but no arguments, no examples, however persuasive or impressive, are sufficient to deter an Indian for an hour from taking the potent draught, which he knows at the time will derange his faculties, reduce him to a level with the brutes, or deprive him of life.

Jacob Jemison, Thomas' second son by his last wife, who is at this time, 1823, twenty-seven or twenty-eight years of age, went to Dartmouth College, in the spring of 1816, for the purpose of receiving an education, where it was said he was an industrious scholar, and made proficiency in the study of the different branches of education to which he attended. Having spent two years in that institution, he returned in the winter of 1818, and is now at Buffalo, (as at time of first publication), where I have understood he contemplates the study of medicine as a profession.

In the month of November, 1811, my husband Hiokatoo, who had been sick of consumption for four years, died at the advanced age of one hundred and three years, as nearly as the time could be estimated. He was the last that remained to me of our family connection, or rather of my old friends with whom I was adopted, except a part of one family, which now resides at Tonawanda, (as at time of first publication). Hiokatoo was buried decently, and had all the insignia of a veteran warrior buried with him; consisting of a war-club, tomahawk and scalping-knife, a powder-flask, flint, a piece of spunk, a small cake, and a cup; and in his best clothing.

According to the Indian mode of burial, the deceased is laid out in his best clothing, and put into a coffin of boards or bark; and with him is deposited, in every instance, a small cup and a cake. Generally two or three candles are put into the coffin, and in a few instances, at the burial of a great man, all his implements of war are buried by the side of the body. The coffin is then closed and carried to the grave. On its being let down, the person who takes the lead of the solemn transaction, or a chief, addresses the dead in a short speech, in which he charges him not to be troubled about himself in his new situation, nor on his journey, and not to trouble his friends, wife, or children, whom he has left; tells him that, if he with strangers on his way, he must inform them what tribe he belongs to, who his relatives are, the situation in which he left them; and that, having done this, he must keep on till he arrives at the good fields in the country of Nauwaneu; that, when he arrives there he will see all his ancestors and personal friends that have gone before him, who, together with all the chiefs of celebrity, will receive him joyfully, and furnish him with every article of perpetual happiness.

The grave is now filled and left till evening, when some of the nearest relatives of the dead build a fire at the head of it, near which they sit till morning. In this way they continue to practice nine successive nights, when, believing that their departed friend has arrived at the end of his journey, they discontinue their attention. During this time the relatives of the deceased are not allowed to dance.

Formerly, frolics were held for the dead, after the expiration of nine days, at which all the squaws got drunk; and those were the only occasions on which they were intoxicated: but lately those are discontinued, and squaws feel no delicacy in getting inebriated.[2]

---

2. The religious system of the Iroquois taught that it was a journey from earth to heaven, of many days' duration. Originally it was supposed to be a year, and the period of mourning for the departed was fixed at that term. At its expiration it was customary for the relatives of the deceased to hold a feast—(continued next page),

Hiokatoo was an old man when I first saw him; but he was by no means enervated. During the time of nearly fifty years that I lived with him, I received, according to Indian customs, all the kindness and attention that was my due as his wife. Although war was his trade from his youth till old age and decrepitude stopped his career, he uniformly treated me with tenderness, and never offered an insult.

I have frequently heard him repeat the history of his life from his childhood; and when he came to that part which related to his actions, his bravery, and valour in war; when he spoke of the ambush, the combat, the spoiling of his enemies, and the sacrifice of his victims, his nerves seemed strung with youthful ardour, the warmth of the able warrior seemed to animate his frame, and to produce the heated gestures which he had practiced in middle age. He was a man of tender feelings to his friends, ready and willing to assist them in distress, yet, as a warrior, his cruelties to his enemies perhaps were unparalleled, and will not admit a word of palliation.

---

the soul of the departed having reached heaven, and a state of felicity, there was no longer any cause for mourning. In modern times the mourning period has been reduced to ten days, and the journey of the spirit is now believed to be performed in three. The spirit of the deceased was supposed to hover around the body for a season before it took its final departure; and not until after the expiration of a year, according to the ancient belief, and ten days according to the present, did it become permanently at rest in heaven. A beautiful custom prevailed, in ancient times, of capturing a bird, and freeing it over the grave on the evening of the burial, to bear away the spirit to its heavenly rest. Their notions of the state of the soul when disembodied are vague and diversified; but they all agree that, during the journey, it required the same nourishment as while it dwelt in the body. They, therefore, deposited beside the deceased his bow and arrows, tobacco and pipe, and necessary food for the journey. They also painted the face, and dressed the body in its best apparel. A fire was built upon the grave at night, to enable the spirit to prepare its food. With these tokens of affection, and these superstitious concernments for the welfare of the deceased, the children of the forest performed the burial rites of their departed kindred.—*League of the Iroquois.*

# CHAPTER 11

# Mary's Family Troubles Continue

Being now left a widow in my old age, to mourn the loss of a husband, who had treated me well, and with whom I had raised five children; and having suffered the loss of an affectionate son, I fondly fostered the hope that my melancholy vicissitudes had ended, and that the remainder of my time would be characterized by nothing unpropitious. My children dutiful and kind, lived near me, and apparently nothing obstructed our happiness.

But a short time, however, elapsed, after my husband's death, before my troubles were renewed with redoubled severity.

John's hand having been once stained in the blood of a brother, although acquitted of murder by the chiefs, it was not strange that every person of his acquaintance should shun him, from a fear of his repeating upon them the same ceremony that he had practiced upon Thomas. My son Jesse went to Mount Morris, a few miles from home, on business, in the winter after the death of his father; and it so happened that his brother John was there, who requested Jesse to come home with him. Jesse, fearing that John would commence a quarrel with him on the way, declined the invitation, and tarried over night.

From that time John conceived himself despised by and was highly enraged at the treatment which he had received from him. Very little was said, however, and it all passed off apparently, till sometime in the month of May, 1812; at which time Mr. Robert Whaley, who lived in the town of Castile, within four miles of me, came to my house early on Monday morning, to hire George Chongo, my son-in-law, and John and Jesse, to go that day and help him slide a quantity of boards from the top of the hill to the river, where he calculated to build a raft of them for market.

They all concluded to go with Mr. Whaley, and made ready as soon as possible. But before they set out, I charged them not to drink any whisky; for I was confident that if they did, they would surely have a quarrel, in consequence, of it. They went and worked till almost night, when a quarrel ensued between Chongo and Jesse, in consequence of the whisky which they had drank through the day, which terminated in a battle, and Chongo got whipped.

When Jesse had got through with Chongo, he told Mr. Whaley that he would go home, and directly went off. He, however, went but a few rods, before he stopped and lay down by the side of a log to wait, as was supposed, for company. John, as soon as Jesse was gone, went to Mr. Whaley, with his knife in his hand, and bade him *jogo; i. e.*, be gone; at the same time telling him that Jesse was a bad man. Mr. Whaley, seeing that his countenance exhibited a demon-like malignity, and that he was determined upon something desperate, was alarmed for his own safety, and turned toward home, leaving Chongo on the ground drunk, near to where Jesse had laid, who by this time had got up, and was advancing toward John. Mr. Whaley was soon out of hearing of them; but some of his workmen stayed till it was dark. Jesse came up to John, and said to him, "You want more whisky, and more fighting," and after a few words went at him, to try in the first place to get away his knife. In this he did not succeed, and they parted.

By this time the night had come on, and it was dark. Again they clenched, and at length in their struggle they both fell. John, having his knife in his hand, came under; and in this situation gave Jesse a fatal stab with his knife, and repeated the blows till Jesse, crying out "Brother you have killed me," quit his hold, and settled back upon the ground. Upon hearing this, John left him, came to Thomas' widow's house, told them that he had been fighting with their uncle, whom he killed, and showed them his knife.

Next morning as soon as it was light, Thomas' and John's children came and told me that Jesse was dead in the woods, and also informed me how he came by his death. John soon followed them, and informed me himself of all that had taken place between him and his brother, and seemed to be somewhat sorrowful for his conduct. You can better imagine what my feelings were than I can describe them. My darling son—my youngest child—him on whom I depended—was dead; and I, in my old age, left destitute of a helping hand!

As soon as it was consistent for me, I got Mr. George Jemison (of whom I shall have occasion to speak,) to go with his sleigh to where Jesse was, and bring him home—a distance of three or four miles. My daughter Polly arrived at the fatal spot first; we got there soon after her, though I went the whole distance on foot. By this time, Chongo, who was left on the ground drunk the night before, had become sober, and sensible of the great misfortune which had happened to our family.

I was overcome with grief at the sight of my murdered son, and so far lost the command of myself as to be almost frantic; and those who were present were obliged to hold me from going near him.

On examining the body, it was found that it had received eighteen wounds, so deep and large that it was believed that either of them would have proved mortal. The corpse was carried to my house, and kept till the Thursday following, when it was buried after the manner of burying white people.

Jesse was twenty-seven or eight years old when he was killed. His temper had been uniformly very mild and friendly; and he was inclined to copy after the white people, both in his manners and dress. Although he was naturally temperate, he occasionally became intoxicated; but never was quarrelsome or mischievous. With the white people he was intimate, and learned from them their habits of industry, which he was fond of practicing, especially when my comfort demanded his labour. As I have observed, it is the custom among the Indians for the women to perform all the labour in and out of doors, and I had the whole to do, with the help of my daughters, till Jesse arrived to a sufficient age to assist us. He was disposed to labour in the cornfield, to chop my wood, milk my cows, and attend to any kind of business that would make my task the lighter.

On the account of his having been my youngest child, and so willing to help me, I am sensible that I loved him better than I did either of my other children. After he began to understand my situation, and the means of rendering it more easy, I never wanted for anything that was in his power to bestow; but since his death, as I have had all my labour to perform alone, I have constantly seen hard times.

Jesse shunned the company of his brothers, and the Indians generally and never attended their frolics; and it was supposed that this, together with my partiality for him, were, the causes which excited in John so great a degree of envy that nothing short of death would satisfy it.[1]

---

1. "Soon after the War of 1812, an altercation occurred between David Reese, (who was at that time the government blacksmith for the Senecas, upon the reservation near Buffalo,) and a Seneca Indian called Young King, (continued next page),

which resulted in a severe blow with a scythe, inflicted by Reese, which nearly severed one of the Indian's arms; so near, in fact, that amputation was immediately resorted to. The circumstance created considerable excitement among the Indians, which extended to Gardeau, the then home of the Jemison family. John Jemison headed a party from there, and went to Buffalo, giving out, as he travelled along the road, that he was going to kill Reese. The author saw him on his way, and recollects how well he personated the ideal "Angel of Death." His weapons were the war-club and the tomahawk; red paint was daubed on his swarthy face, and long bunches of horse-hair, coloured red, were dangling from each arm. His warlike appearance was well calculated to give an earnest to his threats. Reese was kept secreted, and thus, in all probability, avoided the fate that even kindred had met at the hands of John Jemison."—Turner's *History of the Holland Purchase.*

# CHAPTER 12

# Mary's Pretended Cousin, George Jemison

A year or two before the death of my husband, Captain H. Jones sent me word that a cousin of mine was then living on Genesee Flats, by the name of George Jemison; and as he was very poor, thought it advisable for me to go and see him, and take him home to live with me on my land. My Indian friends were pleased to hear that one of my relatives was so near, and also advised me to send for him and his family immediately. I accordingly had him and his family moved into one of my houses, in the month of March, 1810.

He said that he was my father's brother's son—that his father did not leave Europe till after the French war in America, and that when he did come over, he settled in Pennsylvania, where he died. George had no personal knowledge of my father; but from information, was confident that the relationship which he claimed between himself and me actually existed. Although I had never before heard of my father having had but one brother, (him who was killed at Fort Necessity,) I knew that he might have had others; and, as the story of George carried with it a probability that it was true, I received him as a kinsman, and treated him with every degree of friendship which his situation demanded.

I found that he was destitute of the means of subsistence, and in debt to the amount of seventy dollars, without the ability to pay one cent. He had no cow, and finally was completely poor. I paid his debts to the amount of seventy-two dollars, and bought him a cow, for which I paid twenty dollars; and a sow and pigs, that I paid eight dollars for. I also paid sixteen dollars for pork which I gave him, and furnished him with other provisions and furniture; so that his family was comfortable. As he was destitute of a team, I furnished him with one, and also supplied him with tools for farming. In addition to all this, I let him have one of Thomas' cows, for two seasons.

My only object in mentioning his poverty, and the articles with which I supplied him, is to show how ungrateful a person can be for favours received, and how soon they will apparently forget charitable deeds, and conspire against the interest of a benefactor.

Thus furnished with the necessary implements of husbandry, a good team, and as much land as he could till, he commenced farming on my flats, and for some time laboured well. At length, however, he got an idea that if he could become the owner of a part of my reservation, he could live more easily, and certainly be more rich; and accordingly set himself about laying a plan to obtain it, in the easiest manner possible.

I supported Jemison and his family eight years, and probably should have continued to have done so to this day, had it not been for the occurrence of the following circumstance:

When he had lived with me some six or seven years, a friend of mine told me that as Jemison was my cousin, and very poor, I ought to give him a piece of land, that he might have something whereon to live that he could call his own. My friend and Jemison were then together at my house, prepared to complete a bargain. I asked how much land he wanted? Jemison said that he should be glad to receive his own field, (as he called it,) containing about fourteen acres, and a new one that contained twenty-six. I observed to them that as I was incapable of transacting business of that nature, I would wait till Mr. Thomas Clute, (a neighbour on whom I depended,) should return from Albany, before I should do anything about it. To this Jemison replied, that if I waited till Mr. Clute returned, he should not get the land at all; and appeared very anxious to have the business closed without delay. On my part, I felt disposed to give him land; but knowing my ignorance of writing, feared to do it alone, lest they might include as much land as they pleased, without my knowledge.

They then read the deed, which my friend had prepared before he came from home, describing a piece of land by certain bounds that were a specified number of chains and links from each other. Not understanding the length of a chain or link, I described the bounds of a piece of land that I intended Jemison should have, which they said was just the same that the deed contained, and no more. I told them that the deed must not include a lot that was called the Steele place, and they assured me that it did not. Upon this—putting confidence in them both—I signed the deed to George Jemison, containing, and conveying to him, as I supposed, forty acres of land. The deed being completed, they charged me never to mention the bargain which I had then made to any person; because if I did, they said, it would spoil the contract. The whole matter was afterward disclosed; when it was found that that deed, instead of containing only forty acres, contained four hundred, and that one-half of it actually belonged to my friend, as it had been given to him by Jemison, as a reward for his trouble in procuring the deed in the fraudulent manner above mentioned.

My friend, however, by the advice of some well-disposed people, a while afterward gave up his claim. George Jemison, however, held on to his claim; but knowing that he had no title to the land—even if I had then possessed the power of conveying, which it since appears that I did not—as the deed was void, having been obtained by falsehood and fraud, he dared not press his claims under it himself, for fear of being punished for a misdemeanour. He therefore sold his claim for a mere trifle, to a gentleman in the south part of Genesee County, who lost that trifle, whatever it was. But had Jemison been content with getting a deed of the forty acres which I intended to have given him, and not have undertaken to defraud me out of more, I should have made his title good to that land when I did receive the power; and the forty acres would have been worth to him from forty to fifty dollars per acre. This is another proof that, in all cases, "*honesty is the best policy.*"

Sometime after the death of my son Thomas, one of his sons went to Jemison to get the cow that I had let him have for two years; but Jemison refused to let her go, and struck the boy so violent a blow as to almost kill him. Jemison then ran to Jellis Clute, Esq., to procure a warrant to take the boy; but Young King, an Indian chief, went down to Squawky Hill, to Mr. Clute's, and settled the affair, by Jemison's agreeing never to use that club again. Having satisfactorily found out the unfriendly disposition of my cousin toward me, I got him off my premises as soon as possible.

I am now confident that George Jemison is not my cousin, but that he claimed relationship only to obtain assistance.

# CHAPTER 13

# John Jemison Murdered

Trouble seldom comes single. While George Jemison was busily engaged in his pursuit of wealth at my expense, another event of a much more serious nature occurred, which added greatly to my afflictions, and consequently destroyed, at least a part of the happiness that I had anticipated was laid up in the archives of Providence, to be dispensed on my old age.

My son John, was a doctor, considerably celebrated amongst the Indians of various tribes, for his skill in curing their diseases, by the administration of roots and herbs, which he gathered in the forests, and other places where they had been planted by the hand of nature.

In the month of April, or first of May, 1817, he was called upon to go to Buffalo, Cattaraugus and Allegany, to cure some who were sick. He went, and was absent about two months. When he returned, he observed the Great Slide of the bank of Genesee River, a short distance above my house, which had taken place during his absence; and conceiving that circumstance to be ominous of his own death, called at his sister Nancy's, told her that he should live but a few days, and wept bitterly at the near approach of his dissolution. Nancy endeavoured to persuade him that his trouble was imaginary, and that he ought not to be affected by a fancy which was visionary. Her arguments were ineffectual, and afforded no alleviation to his mental sufferings.

From his sister's, he went to his own house, where he stayed only two nights, and then went to Squawky Hill to procure money, with which to purchase flour for the use of his family.

While at Squawky Hill he got into the company of two Squawky Hill Indians, whose names were Doctor and Jack, with whom he drank freely, and in the afternoon had a desperate quarrel, in which his opponents, (as it was afterwards understood,) agreed to kill him. The quarrel ended, and each appeared to be friendly. John bought some spirits, of which they all drank, and then set out for home. John and an Allegany Indian were on horseback, and Doctor and Jack were on foot. It was dark when they set out. They had not proceeded far, when Doctor and Jack commenced another quarrel with John, clenched and dragged him off his horse, and then with a stone gave him so severe a blow on his head, that some of his brains were discharged from the wound. The Allegany Indian, fearing that his turn would come next, fled for safety as fast as possible.

John recovered a little from the shock he had received, and endeavoured to get to an old hut that stood near; but they caught him, and with an axe cut his throat, and beat out his brains, so that when he was found the contents of his skull were lying on his arms.

Some squaws, who heard the uproar, ran to find out the cause of it; but before they had time to offer their assistance, the murderers drove them into a house, and threatened to take their lives if they did not stay there, or if they made any noise.

Next morning, Esq. Clute sent me word that John was dead, and also informed me of the means by which his life was taken. A number of people went from Gardeau to where the body lay, and Doctor Levi Brundridge brought it up home, where the funeral was attended after the manner of the white people. Mr. Benjamin Luther, and Mr. William Wiles, preached a sermon, and performed the funeral services; and myself and family followed the corpse to the grave as mourners. I had now buried my three sons, who had been snatched from me by the hands of violence, when I least expected it.

Although John had taken the life of his two brothers, and caused me unspeakable trouble and grief, his death made a solemn impression upon my mind, and seemed, in addition to my former misfortunes, enough to bring down my grey hairs with sorrow to the grave. Yet, on a second thought, I could not mourn for him as I had for my other sons, because I knew that his death was just, and what he had deserved for a long time, from the hand of justice.

John's vices were so great and so aggravated, that I have nothing to say in his favour yet, as a mother, I pitied him while he lived, and have ever felt a great degree of sorrow for him, because of his bad conduct.

From his childhood, he carried something in his features indicative of an evil disposition, that would result in the perpetration of enormities of some kind; and it was the opinion and saying of Ebenezer Allen,

THE MURDER OF ONE OF HER SONS BY HIS BROTHER.

that he would be a bad man, and be guilty of some crime deserving of death. There is no doubt but what the thoughts of murder rankled in his breast, and disturbed his mind even in his sleep; for he dreamed that he had killed Thomas for a trifling offence, and thereby forfeited his own life. Alarmed at the revelation, and fearing that he might in some unguarded moment destroy his brother, he went to the Black Chief, to whom he told the dream, and expressed his fears that the vision would be verified. Having related the dream, together with his feelings on the subject, he asked for the best advice that his old friend was capable of giving, to prevent so sad an event. The Black Chief, with his usual promptitude, told him, that from the nature of the dream, he was fearful that something serious would take place between him and Thomas; and advised him by all means to govern his temper, and avoid any quarrel which in future he might see arising, especially if Thomas was a party. John, however, did not keep the good counsel of the chief; for soon after he killed Thomas, as I have related.

John left two wives with whom he had lived at the same time, and raised nine children. His widows are now living at Caneadea with their father, and keep their children with, and near them, (as at time of first publication). His children are tolerably white, and have got light coloured hair. John died about the last day of June, 1817, aged 54 years.

Doctor and Jack, having finished their murderous design, fled before they could be apprehended, and lay six weeks in the woods back of Canisteo. They then returned and sent me some *wampum* by Chongo, (my son-in-law,) and Sun-ge-waw[1] that is Big Kettle, expecting that I would pardon them, and suffer them to live as they had done with their tribe. I however, would not accept their *wampum*, but returned it with a request, that, rather than have them killed, they would run away and keep out of danger.

On their receiving back the *wampum*, they took my advice, and prepared to leave their country and people immediately. Their relatives accompanied them a short distance on their journey, and when about to part, their old uncle, the Tall Chief, addressed them in the

---

1. The greatest of all human crimes, murder, was punished with death; but the act was open to condonation. Unless the family were appeased, the murderer, as with the ancient Greeks, was given up to their private vengeance. They could take his life wherever they found him, even after the lapse of years, without being held accountable. A present of white *wampum* sent on the part of the murderer to the family of his victim, when accepted, forever obliterated the memory of the transaction.—
*League of the Iroquois.*

following pathetic and sentimental speech:

> Friends, hear my voice! When the Great Spirit made Indians, he made them all good, and gave them good cornfields; good rivers, well stored with fish; good forests, filled with game and good bows and arrows. But very soon each wanted more than his share, and Indians quarrelled with Indians, and some were killed, and others were wounded. Then the Great Spirit made a very good word, and put it in every Indians breast, to tell us when we have done good, or when we have done bad—and that word has never told a lie.
>
> Friends! whenever you have stole, or got drunk, or lied, that good word has told you that you were bad Indians, and made you afraid of good Indians; and made you ashamed and look down.
>
> Friends! your crime is greater than all those; you have killed an Indian in a time of peace; and made the wind hear his groans, and the earth drink his blood. You are bad Indians! Yes, you are very bad Indians; and what can you do? If you go into the woods to live alone, the ghost of John Jemison will follow you, crying, blood! blood! and will give you no peace! If you go to the land of your nation, there that ghost will attend you, and say to your relatives, see my murderers! If you plant, it will blast your corn; if you hunt, it will scare your game; and when you are asleep, its groans, and the sight of an avenging tomahawk, will awake you!
>
> What can you do? Deserving of death, you cannot live here; and to fly from your country, to leave all your relatives, and to abandon all that you have known to be pleasant and dear, must be keener than an arrow, more bitter than gall, more terrible than death! And how must we feel? Your path will be muddy; the woods will be dark; the lightnings will glance down the trees by your side, and you will start at every sound! peace has left you, and you must be wretched.
>
> Friends, hear me, and take my advice. Return with us to your homes. Offer to the Great Spirit your best *wampum*, and try to be good Indians! And, if those whom you have bereaved shall claim your lives as their only satisfaction, surrender them cheerfully, and die like good Indians. And—

Here Jack, highly incensed, interrupted the old man, and bade him stop speaking or he would take his life. Affrighted at the appearance of so much desperation, the company hastened towards home, and left Doctor and Jack to consult their own feelings.

As soon as they were alone, Jack said to Doctor, "I had rather die here, than leave my country and friends! Put the muzzle of your rifle into my mouth, and I will put the muzzle of mine into yours, and at a given signal we will discharge them, and rid ourselves at once of all the troubles under which we now labour, and satisfy the claims which justice holds against us."

Doctor heard the proposition, and after a moment's pause, made the following reply:

I am as sensible as you can be of the unhappy situation in which we have placed ourselves. We are bad Indians. We have forfeited our lives, and must expect in some way to atone for our crime: but, because we are bad and miserable, shall we make ourselves worse? If we were now innocent, and in a calm reflecting moment should kill ourselves, that act would make us bad, and deprive us of our share of the good hunting in the land where our fathers have gone! What would Little Beard say to us on our arrival at his cabin? He would say, 'Bad Indians! Cowards! You were afraid to wait till we wanted your help! Go (*jogo*) to where snakes will lie in your path; where the panthers will starve you, by devouring the venison; and where you will be naked and suffer with the cold! *Jogo*, (go,) none but the brave and good Indians live here!' I cannot think of performing an act that will add to my wretchedness. It is hard enough for me to suffer here, and have good hunting hereafter—worse to lose the whole.

Upon this, Jack withdrew his proposal. They went on about two miles, and then turned about and came home. Guilty and uneasy, they lurked about Squawky Hill near a fortnight, and then went to Cattaraugus, and were gone six weeks. When they came back, Jack's wife earnestly requested him to remove his family to Tonnewonta; but he remonstrated against her project, and utterly declined going. His wife and family, however, tired of the tumult by which they were surrounded, packed up their effects in spite of what he could say, and went off.

Jack deliberated a short time upon the proper course for himself to pursue, and finally, rather than leave his old home, he ate a large quantity of muskrat root, and died in ten or twelve hours. His family being immediately notified of his death, returned to attend the burial, and is yet living at Squawky Hill, (as at time of first publication).

Nothing was ever done with Doctor, who continued to live quietly at Squawky Hill till sometime in the year 1819, when he died of consumption.

CHAPTER 14

# The Hardships of Her Life

In the year 1816, Micah Brooks, Esq., of Bloomfield, Ontario county, and Jellis Clute, Esq., of Leicester, began to negotiate with me for the purchase of a part of my land, as it lay in an unproductive state to me. Many obstacles presented themselves in the transaction of the business. In the first place, it was objected that I was not a citizen of the United States, and could not legally convey land, without a special act of the legislature. To surmount this difficulty, Messrs. Brooks and Clute procured a special act of the legislature of this state to be passed, conferring naturalization on me, and confirming my title to the land as far as that body could effect it. It was then discovered that the assent of the chiefs of the Seneca Nation must be had to the conveyance, and that the proceedings to obtain such assent must be in council, under the superintendence of a commissioner appointed by the President of the United States.

After much delay and vexation in ascertaining what was necessary to be clone to effect the object in a legal manner, and having consulted my children and friends, in the winter of 1822-3, I agreed with Messrs. Brooks and Clute, that if they would get the chiefs of our nation, and a United States commissioner of Indian lands, to meet in Moscow, Livingston county, N.Y., I would sell to them all my right and title to the Gardeau reservation, containing 17,927 acres, with the exception of a tract for my own benefit, two miles long and one mile wide, lying on Genesee River, where I should choose it; and also reserving a lot I had promised to give to Thomas, Clute, as a recompense for his faithful guardianship over me and my property for a long time.

The arrangement was agreed to, and the council assembled on the third or fourth day of September last, at the place appointed, consisting of Major Carrol, Judge Howell, and N. Gorham, acting for and in behalf of the United States government; Jasper Parish, Indian agent; Horatio Jones, interpreter; and a large number of Seneca chiefs. The bargain was assented to unanimously, and a deed was executed and delivered by me and upward of twenty chiefs, conveying all my right and title to the Gardeau reservation, except the reservations before mentioned, to Henry B. Gibson, Micah Brooks, and Jellis Clute, their heirs and assigns forever.

The tract which I reserved for myself begins at the centre of the Great Slide; thence running west one mile; thence north two miles; thence east about a mile to the river: and thence running southerly up the river; and bounding on the west bank to the place of beginning.

In consideration of the before-mentioned sale to Messrs. Gibson, Brooks, and Clute, among other things, they bound themselves, their heirs, assigns, etc., to pay to me, my heirs or successors, three hundred dollars a year forever.

When I review my life, the privations that I have suffered, the hardships I have endured, the vicissitudes I have passed, and the complete revolution that I have experienced in my manner of living; when I consider my reduction from a civilized to a savage state, and the various steps by which that process has been effected, and that my life has been prolonged, and my health and reason spared, it seems a miracle that I am unable to account for, and is a tragical medley that I hope will never be repeated. The bare loss of liberty is but a mere trifle, when compared with the circumstances that necessarily attend, and are inseparably connected with it. It is the recollection of what we once were, of the friends, the home we have left, and the pleasures that we have lost; the anticipation of misery, the appearance of wretchedness, the anxiety for freedom, the hope of release, the devising of means of escaping, and the vigilance with which we watch our keepers, that constitute the nauseous dregs of the bitter cup of slavery.

I am sensible, however, that no one can pass from a state of freedom to that of slavery, and in the latter situation rest perfectly contented; but as everyone knows that great exertions of the mind tend directly to debilitate the body, it will appear obvious that we ought, when confined, to exert all our faculties to promote our present comfort, and let future days provide their own sacrifices. In regard to ourselves, just as we feel, we are.

For the preservation of my life to the present time I am indebted to an excellent constitution, with which I have been blessed in as great a degree as any other person. After I arrived to years of understanding, the care of my own health was one of my principal studies; and by avoiding exposures to wet and cold, by temperance in eating, abstaining from the use of spirits, and shunning the excesses to which I was frequently exposed, I effected my object beyond what I expected. I have never once been sick till within a year or two, only as I have related.

Spirits and tobacco I have never used, and I have never once attended an Indian frolic. When I was taken prisoner, and for some time after that, spirits were unknown among the Indians; and when they were first introduced, it was in small quantities, and used only by, the Indians; so that it was a long time before the Indian Women began even to taste it.

After the French war, for a number of years it was the practice of the Indians of our tribe to send to Niagara and get two or three kegs of rum—in all six or eight gallons—and hold a frolic as long as it lasted. When the rum was brought to the town, all the Indians collected, and before a drop was drank, gave all their knives, tomahawks, guns, and other instruments of war, to one Indian, whose business it was to bury them in a private place, keep them concealed, and remain perfectly sober till the frolic was ended. Having thus divested themselves, they commenced drinking, and continued their frolic till every drop was consumed. If any of them became quarrelsome, or got to fighting, those who were sober enough bound them upon the ground, where they were obliged to lie till they got sober, and then were unbound. When the fumes of the spirits had left the company, the sober Indian returned to each the instruments with which they had entrusted him, and all went home satisfied. A frolic of that kind was held but once a year, and that at the time the Indians quit their hunting, and came in with their deer-skins.

In those frolics the women never participated. Soon after the Revolutionary War, however, spirits became common in our tribe, and have been used indiscriminately by both sexes; though there are not so frequent instances of intoxication among the squaws as among the Indians.

To the introduction and use of that baneful article which has made such devastation in our tribes, and threatens the extinction of our people, (the Indians,) I can with the greatest propriety impute the whole of my misfortune in losing my three sons. But as I have before observed, not even the love of life will restrain an Indian from sipping the poison that he knows will destroy him. The voice of nature, the rebukes of reason, the advice of parents, the expostulations of friends, and the numerous instances of sudden death, are all insufficient to restrain an Indian who has once experienced the exhilarating and inebriating effects of spirits, from seeking his grave in the bottom of the bottle.

My strength has been great for a woman of my size; otherwise I must long ago have died under the burdens which I was obliged to carry. I learned to carry loads on my back, supported by a strap placed across my forehead, soon after my captivity; and continue to carry in the same way. Upward of thirty years ago, and with the help of my young children, I backed all the boards that were used about my house from Allen's mill at the outlet of Silver Lake, a distance of five miles. I have planted, hoed, and harvested corn every season but one since I was taken prisoner. Even this present fall, 1823, I have husked my corn, and backed it into the house.

The first cow that I ever owned, I bought of a squaw sometime after the Revolution. It had been stolen from the enemy. I had owned it but a few days when it fell into a hole, and almost died before we could get it out. After this, the squaw wanted to be recanted; but as I would not give up the cow, I gave her money enough to make, when added to the sum which I paid her at first, thirty-five dollars. Cows were plenty on the Ohio, when I lived there, and of good quality.

For provisions, I have never suffered since I came upon the flats; nor have I ever been indebted to any other hands than my own for the plenty that I have shared.

I have never been accused of many vices. Some of my children had light-brown hair, and tolerably fair skin, which used to make some people say that I stole them; yet, as I was ever conscious of my own constancy, I never thought that anyone really believed that I was guilty of adultery. It was believed for a long time, by some of our people, that I was a great witch; but they were unable to prove my guilt, and consequently I escaped the certain doom of those who are convicted of that crime, which, by the Indians, is considered as heinous as murder.

The term in the Seneca language meaning witch applies equally to both sexes. They believe that there are many witches, and that, next to the author of evil, they are the greatest scourge to the people. The term denotes a person to whom the evil deity has delegated power to inflict diseases, cause death, blast corn, bring bad weather, and, in short, to cause almost any calamity to which they are liable. With this impression, and believing that it is their actual duty to destroy, as far as is in their power, every source of unhappiness, it has been a custom among them from time immemorial, to destroy every one that' they could convict of so heinous a crime; and in fact there is no reprieve from the sentence.

Executions for witchcraft are not an uncommon occurrence. More or less, charged with being witches, have been executed in almost every year I have lived on the Genesee. Many, on being suspected, made their escape; while others, before they were aware of being implicated, have been apprehended and brought to trial. A number of years ago, an Indian chased a squaw, near Little Beard's Town, and caught her; but on account of her great strength she got away. The Indian, vexed and disappointed, went home, and the next day reported that he saw her have fire in her mouth, and that she was a witch. Upon this she was apprehended and killed immediately. She was Bigtree's cousin. I was present at that execution, and also saw another who had been convicted of being a witch, killed, and thrown into the river. Thus, from the most trifling causes, thousands have lost their lives through the superstitious fanaticism of the pagan Indians, for they will not "suffer a witch to live."

I have been the mother of eight children;—three of whom are now living,—and I have at this time thirty-nine grandchildren, and fourteen great-grandchildren all living in the neighbourhood of Genesee River, and at Buffalo, (as at time of first publication).

I live in my own house, and on my own land, with my youngest daughter, Polly, who is married to George Chongo, and has three children.

My daughter Nancy, who is married to Billy Green, lives about eighty rods south of my house, and has seven children.

My other daughter, Betsey, is married to John Green, has children, and resides eighty rods north of my house.

Thus situated in the midst of my children, I expect I shall soon leave the world, and make room for the rising generation. I feel the weight of years with which I am loaded, and am sensible of my daily failure, in seeing, hearing, and strength; but my only anxiety is for my family. If my family will live happily, and I can be exempted from trouble while I have to stay. I feel as though I could lay down in peace, a life that has been checked in almost every hour, with troubles of a deeper dye than are commonly experienced by mortals.

# Life of Hi-ok-a-too

Hiokatoo was born on the banks of the Susquehanna, in the year 1708, in one of the tribes of the Senecas which inhabited that region at the time of his birth. He was own cousin to Farmer's Brother, a chief who had been justly celebrated for his worth. Their mothers were sisters, and it was through the influence of Farmer's Brother that I became Hiokatoo's wife.

In early life, Hiokatoo showed signs of thirst for blood, by attending only to the art of war, in the use of the tomahawk and scalping knife; and in practising cruelties upon everything that chanced to fall into his hands, which was susceptible of pain. In that way he learned to use his implements of war effectually, and at the same time blunted all those fine feelings and tender sympathies that are naturally excited, by hearing or seeing, a fellow being in distress. He could inflict the most excruciating tortures upon his enemies, and prided himself upon his fortitude, in having performed the most barbarous ceremonies and tortures, without the least degree of pity or remorse. Thus qualified, when very young he was initiated into scenes of carnage, by being engaged in the wars that prevailed amongst the Indian tribes.

When he was a young man, there lived in the same tribe with him an old Indian warrior who was a great counsellor, by the name of Buck-in-je-hil-ish. Buckinjehullish having with great fatigue, attended the council when it was deliberating upon war, declared that the wise men and the warriors had to do the fighting. This speech exasperated his countrymen to such a degree that he was apprehended and tried for a witch, on the account of his having lived to so an advanced age; and because he could not show some reason why he had not died before, he was sentenced to be tomahawked by a boy on the

1. This chapter was added by Ebenezer Mix

spot, which was accordingly done.

In the year 1731, Hiokatoo was appointed a runner, to assist in collecting an army to go against the Catawbas, Cherokees and other southern Indians. A large army was collected, and after a long and fatiguing march, met its enemies in what was then called the "low, dark and bloody lands," near the mouth of Red River, in what is now called the state of Tennessee, at or near the site of the present village of Clarksville, in the county of Montgomery. The Catawbas and their associates, had, by some means, been apprised of their approach, and lay in ambush to take them at once, when they should come within their reach, and destroy the whole army. The northern Indians, with their usual sagacity, discovered the situation of their enemies, rushed upon the ambuscade and massacred twelve hundred on the spot. The battle continued for two days and two nights, with the utmost severity, in which the northern Indians were victorious, and so far succeeded in destroying the Catawbas that they at that time ceased to be a nation. The victors suffered an immense loss in killed; but gained the hunting ground, which was their grand object, though the Cherokees would not give it up in a treaty, or consent to make peace. Bows and arrows, at that time were generally used as implements of Indian warfare, although a few guns had been introduced.

From that time he was engaged in a number of battles in which, as in the Catawba and Cherokee wars, Indians only were engaged, and that made fighting his business, till the commencement of the French war. In those battles he took a number of Indians prisoners, whom he killed by tying them to trees and then setting small Indian boys to shooting at them with arrows, till death finished the misery of the sufferers; a process that frequently took two days for its completion!

During the French war he was in every battle that was fought on the Susquehannah and Ohio Rivers; and was so fortunate as never to have been taken prisoner.

At Braddock's defeat he took two white prisoners, and burnt them alive in a fire of his own kindling.

In 1777, he was in the battle at Fort Freeland, in Northumberland county, Penn. The fort contained a great number of women and children, and was defended only by a small garrison. The force that went against it consisted of one hundred British regulars, commanded by a Colonel McDonald, and three hundred Indians under Hiokatoo. After a short but bloody engagement, the fort was surrendered; the women and children were sent under an escort to the next fort below, and the men and boys taken off by a party of British to the general Indian encampment. As soon as the fort had capitulated and the firing had ceased, Hiokatoo with the help of a few Indians tomahawked every wounded American while earnestly begging with uplifted hands for quarters.

The massacre was but just finished when Captains Dougherty and Boon arrived with a reinforcement to assist the garrison. On their arriving in sight of the fort they saw that it had surrendered, and that an Indian was holding the flag. This so much inflamed Captain Dougherty that he left his command, stepped forward and shot the Indian at the first fire. Another took the flag, and had no sooner got it erected than Dougherty dropped him as he had the first. A third presumed to hold it, who was also shot down by Dougherty. Hiokatoo, exasperated at the sight of such bravery, sallied out with a party of his Indians, and killed Captains Dougherty, Boon, and fourteen men, at the first fire. The remainder of the two companies escaped by taking to flight, and soon arrived at the fort which they had left but a few hours before.

In an expedition that went out against Cherry Valley and the neighbouring settlements, Captain David, a Mohawk Indian, was first, and Hiokatoo the second in command. The force consisted of several hundred Indians, who were determined on mischief, and the destruction of the whites. A continued series of wantonness and barbarity characterized their career, for they plundered and burnt everything that came in their way, and killed a number of persons, among whom were several infants, whom Hiokatoo butchered or dashed upon the stones with his own hands. Besides the instances which have been mentioned, he was in a number of parties during the Revolutionary War, where he ever acted a conspicuous part.

The Indians having removed the seat of their depredations and war to the frontiers of Pennsylvania, Ohio, Kentucky and the neighbouring territories, assembled a large force at Upper Sandusky, their place of general rendezvous, from whence they went out to the various places which they designed to sacrifice.

Tired of the desolating scenes that were so often witnessed, and feeling a confidence that the savages might be subdued, and an end put to their crimes, the American government raised a regiment, consisting of 300 volunteers, for the purpose of dislodging them from their cantonment and preventing further barbarities. Colonel William Crawford and Lieutenant Colonel David Williamson—men who had been thoroughly tried and approved—were commissioned by General Washington to take the command of a service that seemed all-important to the welfare of the country. In the month of July, 1782, well-armed and provided with a sufficient quantity of provision, this regiment made an expeditious march through the wilderness to Upper Sandusky, where, as had been anticipated, they found the Indians assembled in full force at their encampment, prepared to receive an attack.

As Colonel Crawford and his brave band advanced, and when they had got within a short distance from the town, they were met by a white man, with a flag of truce from the Indians, who proposed to Colonel Crawford that if he would surrender himself and his men to the Indians, their lives should be spared; but, that if they persisted in their undertaking, and attacked the town, they should all be massacred to a man.

Crawford, while hearing the proposition, attentively surveyed its bearer, and recognized in his features one of his former schoolmates and companions, with whom he was perfectly acquainted, by the name of Simon Gurty. Gurty, but a short time before this, had been a soldier in the American army, in the same regiment with Crawford; but on the account of his not having received the promotion that he expected, he became disaffected, swore an eternal war with his countrymen, fled to the Indians, and joined them, as a leader well qualified to conduct them to where they could satiate their thirst for blood, upon the innocent, unoffending and defenceless settlers. Crawford sternly inquired of the traitor if his name was not Simon Gurty; and being answered in the affirmative, he informed him that he despised the offer which he had made; and that he would not surrender his army unless he should be compelled to do so, by a superior force.

Gurty returned, and Crawford immediately commenced an engagement that lasted till night, without the appearance of victory on either side, when the firing ceased, and the combatants on both sides retired to take refreshment, and to rest through the night. Crawford encamped in the woods near half a mile from the town, where, after the sentinels were placed, and each had taken his ration, they slept on their arms, that they might be instantly ready in case they should be attacked. The stillness of death hovered over the little army, and sleep relieved the whole, except the wakeful sentinels who vigilantly attended to their duty. But what was their surprise, when they found late in the night, that they were surrounded by the Indians on every side, except a narrow space between them and the town? Every man was under arms, and the officers instantly consulted each other on the best method of escaping; for they saw that to fight, would be useless, and that to surrender, would be death.

Crawford proposed a retreat through the ranks of the enemy in an opposite direction from the town, as being the most sure course to take. Lieutenant Colonel Williamson advised to march directly through the town, where there appeared to be no Indians, and the fires were yet burning.

There was no time or place for debates: Colonel Crawford, with sixty followers retreated on the route that he had proposed by attempting to rush through the enemy; but they had no sooner got amongst the Indians, than every man was killed or taken prisoner! Amongst the prisoners, were Colonel Crawford, and Doctor Knight, surgeon of the regiment.

Lieutenant Colonel Williamson, with the remainder of the regiment, together with the wounded, set out at the same time that Crawford did, went through the town without losing a man, and by the help of good guides arrived at their homes in safety.

The next day after the engagement the Indians disposed of all their prisoners to the different tribes, except Colonel Crawford and Doctor Knight; but those unfortunate men were reserved for a more cruel destiny. A council was immediately held on Sandusky Plains, consisting of all the chiefs and warriors, ranged in their customary order, in a circular form; and Crawford and Knight were brought forward and seated in the centre of the circle.

The council being opened, the chiefs began to examine Crawford on various subjects relative to the war. At length they enquired who conducted the military operations of the American army on the Ohio and Susquehannah Rivers, during the year before; and who had led that army against them with so much skill and so uniform success? Crawford very honestly and without suspecting any harm from his reply promptly answered that he was the man who had led his countrymen to victory, who had driven the enemy from the settlements, and by that means had procured a great degree of happiness to many of his fellow-citizens. Upon hearing this, a chief, who had lost a son in the year before, in a battle where Colonel Crawford commanded, left his station in the council, stepped to Crawford, blacked his face, and at the same time told him that the next day he should be burnt.

The council was immediately dissolved on its hearing the sentence from the chief, and the prisoners were taken off the ground, and kept in custody through the night. Crawford now viewed his fate as sealed; and despairing of ever returning to his home or his country, only dreaded the tediousness of death, as commonly inflicted by the savages, and earnestly hoped that he might be despatched at a single blow.

Early the next morning, the Indians assembled at the place of execution, and Crawford was led to the post—the goal of savage torture, to which he was fastened. The post was a stick of timber placed firmly in the ground, having an arm framed in at the top, and extending some six or eight feet from it, like the arm of a sign post. A pile of wood containing about two cords, lay a few feet from the place where he stood, which he was informed was to be kindled into a fire that would burn him alive, as many had been burnt on the same spot, who had been much less deserving than himself.

Gurty stood and supposedly looked on the preparations that were making for the funeral of one his former playmates; a hero by whose side he had fought; of a man whose valour had won laurels which, if he could have returned, would have been strewed upon his grave, by his grateful countrymen. Dreading the agony that he saw he was about to feel, Crawford used every argument which his perilous situation could suggest to prevail upon Gurty to ransom him at any price, and deliver him, as it was in his power, from savages, and their torments. Gurty heard his prayers, and expostulations, and saw his tears with indifference, and finally told the forsaken victim that he would not procure him a moment's respite, nor afford him the most trifling assistance.

The colonel was then bound, stripped naked and tied by his wrists to the arm, which extended horizontally from the post, in such a manner that his arms were extended over his head, with his feet just standing upon the ground. This being done, the savages placed the wood in a circle around him at the distance of a few feet, in order that his misery might be protracted to the greatest length, and then kindled it in a number of places at the same time. The flames arose and the scorching heat became almost insupportable. Again he prayed to Gurty in all the anguish of his torment, to rescue him from the fire, or shoot him dead upon the spot. A demoniac smile suffused the countenance of Gurty, while he calmly replied to the dying suppliant, that he had no pity for his sufferings; but that he was then satisfying that spirit of revenge, which for a long time he had hoped to have an opportunity to wreak upon him.

111

Nature being almost exhausted from the intensity of the heat, he settled down a little, when a squaw threw coals of fire and embers upon him, which made him groan most piteously, while the whole camp rung with exultation. During the execution they manifested all the ecstasy of a complete triumph. Poor Crawford soon died and was entirely consumed.

Thus ended the life of a patriot and hero, who had been an intimate with General Washington, and who shared in an eminent degree the confidence of that great, good man, to whom, in the time of revolutionary perils, the sons of legitimate freedom looked with a degree of faith in his mental resources, unequalled in the history of the world.

That tragedy being ended, Doctor Knight was informed that on the next day he should be burnt in the same manner that his comrade Crawford had been, at Lower Sandusky. Hiokatoo, who out had been a leading chief in the battle with, and in the execution of Crawford, painted Doctor Knight's face black, and then bound and gave him up to two able bodied Indians to conduct to the place of execution.

They set off with him immediately, and travelled till towards evening, when they halted to encamp till morning. The afternoon had been very rainy, and the storm still continued, which rendered it very difficult for the Indians to kindle a fire. Knight observing the difficulty under which they laboured, made them to understand by signs, that if they would unbind him, he would assist them.—They, accordingly unbound him, and he soon succeeded in making a fire by the application of small dry stuff which he was at considerable trouble to procure. While the Indians were warming themselves, the doctor continued to gather wood to last through the night, and in doing this, he found a club which he placed in a situation from whence he could take it conveniently whenever an opportunity should present itself in which he could use it effectually.

The Indians continued warming, till at length the doctor saw that they had placed themselves in a favourable position for the execution of his design, when, stimulated by the love of life, he cautiously took his club and at two blows knocked them both down. Determined to finish the work of death which he had so well begun, he drew one of their scalping knives, with which he beheaded and scalped them both! He then took a rifle, tomahawk, and some ammunition, and directed his course for home, where he arrived without having experienced any difficulty on his journey.

The next morning, the Indians took the track of their victim and his attendants, to go to Lower Sandusky, and there execute the sentence which they had pronounced upon him. But what was their surprise and disappointment, when they arrived at the place of encampment, where they found their trusty friends scalped and decapitated, and that their prisoner had made his escape. Chagrined beyond measure, they immediately separated, and went in every direction in pursuit of their prey; but after having spent a number of days unsuccessfully, they gave up the chase, and returned to their encampment.

In the time of the French war, in an engagement that took place on the Ohio River, Hiokatoo took a British colonel by the name of Simon Canton, whom he carried to the Indian encampment. A council was held, and the colonel was sentenced to suffer death, by being tied on a wild colt, with his face towards its tail, and then having the colt turned loose to run where it pleased. He was accordingly tied on, and the colt let loose, agreeable to the sentence. The colt run two days, and then returned with its rider yet alive. The Indians, thinking that he would never die in that way, took him off, and made him run the gauntlet three times; but in the last race a squaw knocked him down, and he was supposed to have been dead.

He, however, recovered, and was sold for fifty dollars to a Frenchman, who sent him as a prisoner to Detroit. On the return of the Frenchman to Detroit, the colonel besought him to ransom him, and give, or set him at liberty, with so much warmth, and promised with so much solemnity, to reward him as one of the best of benefactors, if he would let him go, that the Frenchman took his word, and sent him home to his family. The colonel remembered his promise, and in a short time sent his deliverer one hundred and fifty dollars, as a reward for his generosity.

Since the commencement of the Revolutionary War, Hiokatoo has been in seventeen campaigns, four of which were in the Cherokee war. He was so great an enemy to the Cherokees, and so fully determined upon their subjugation, that on his march to their country, he raised his own army for those four campaigns, and commanded it; and also superintended its subsistence. In one of those campaigns, which continued two whole years without intermission, he attacked his enemies on the Mobile, drove them to the country of the Creek Nation, where he continued to harass them, till being tired of war, he returned to his family. He brought home a great number of scalps, which he had taken from the enemy, and ever seemed to possess an unconquerable will that the Cherokees might be utterly destroyed. Towards the close of his last fighting in that country, he took two squaws, whom he sold on his way home for money to defray the expense of his journey.

Hiokatoo was about six feet four or five inches high, large boned, and rather inclined to leanness. He was very stout and active, for a man of his size, for it was said by himself and others, that he had never found an Indian who could keep up with him on a race, or throw him at wrestling. His eye was quick and penetrating; and his voice was of that harsh and powerful kind, which, amongst, Indians, always commands attention. His health had been uniformly good. He never was confined by sickness, till he was attacked with the consumption, four years before his death. And, although he had, from his earliest days, been inured to almost constant fatigue, and exposure to every inclemency of the weather, in the open air he seemed to lose the vigour of the prime of life only by the natural decay occasioned by old age.

# CHAPTER 16

# Ebenezer Allen

Sometime near the close of the Revolutionary War, a white man, by the name of Ebenezer Allen, left his people, in the state of Pennsylvania, on account of some disaffection toward his countrymen, and came to the Genesee River to reside with the Indians. He tarried at Genishau a few days, and came up to Gardeau, where I then resided. He was, apparently, without any business that would support him; but he soon became acquainted with my son Thomas, with whom he hunted for a long time, and made his home with him at my house. Winter came on, and he continued his stay.[1]

When Allen came to my house, I had a white man living on my land, who had a Nanticoke squaw for his wife, with whom he had lived very peaceably; for he was a moderate man commonly, and she was a kind, gentle, cunning creature. It so happened that he had no hay for his cattle; so that in the winter he was obliged to drive them every day perhaps a mile from his house, to let them feed on the rushes, which in those days were so numerous as to nearly cover the ground.

Allen, having frequently seen the squaw in the fall, took the opportunity when her husband was absent with his cows, daily to make her a visit; and in return for his kindnesses she made and gave him a red cap, finished and decorated in the highest Indian style.

The husband had for some considerable length of time felt a degree of jealousy that Allen was trespassing upon his rights, with the consent of his squaw; but when he saw Allen dressed in so fine an Indian cap, and found that his dear Nanticoke had presented it to him, his doubts all left him, and he became so violently enraged that he

---

1. "Ebenezer Allen was no hero, but, rather, a *desperado*. He warred against his own race, country, and colour; and vied with his savage allies in deeds of cruelty and bloodshed. He was a native of New Jersey."—Turner's *History of the Holland Purchase*.

caught her by the hair of her head, dragged her on the ground to my house, a distance of forty rods, and threw her in at the door. Hiokatoo, my husband, exasperated at the sight of so much inhumanity, hastily took down his old tomahawk, which for a while had lain idle, shook it over the cuckold's head, and bade him *jogo* (i. e. go off.) The enraged husband, well knowing that he should feel a blow if he waited to hear the order repeated, instantly retreated, and went down the river to his cattle. We protected the poor Nanticoke woman, and gave her victuals; and Allen sympathized with her in her misfortunes till spring, when her husband came to her, acknowledged his former errors, and that he had abused her without a cause, promised a reformation, and she received him with every mark of a renewal of her affection. They went home lovingly, and soon after removed to Niagara.

The same spring, Allen commenced working my flats, and continued to labour there till after the peace of 1783. He then went to Philadelphia on some business that detained him but a few days, and returned with a horse and some dry goods, which he carried to a place that is now called Mount Morris, where he built or bought a small house.

The British and Indians on the Niagara frontier, dissatisfied with the treaty of peace, were determined, at all hazards, to continue their depredations upon the white settlements which lay between them and Albany. They actually made ready, and were about setting out on an expedition to that effect, when Allen (who by this time understood their system of war) took a belt of *wampum*, which he had fraudulently procured, and carried it as a token of peace from the Indians to the commander of the nearest American military post. The Indians were soon answered by the American officer, that the *wampum* was cordially accepted, and that a continuance of peace was ardently wished for. The Indians, at this, were chagrined and disappointed beyond measure; but as they held the *wampum* to be a sacred thing, they dared not go against the import of its meaning, and immediately buried the hatchet, as it respected the people of the United States, and smoked the pipe of peace.

They, however, resolved to punish Allen for his officiousness in meddling with their national affairs, by presenting the sacred *wampum* without their knowledge; and went about devising means for his detection. A party was accordingly dispatched from Fort Niagara to apprehend him; with orders to conduct him to that post for trial, or for safe keeping, till such time as his fate should be determined upon in a legal manner.

The party came on; but before it arrived at Gardeau, Allen got news of its approach., and fled for safety, leaving the horse and goods that he had brought from Philadelphia an easy prey to his enemies. He had not been long absent when they arrived at Gardeau, where they made diligent search for him till they were satisfied that they could not find him, and then seized the effects which he had left, and returned to Niagara. My son Thomas went with them, with Allen's horse, and carried the goods.

Allen, on finding that his enemies had gone, came back to my house, where he lived as before; but of his return they were soon notified at Niagara, and Nettles, (who married Priscilla Ramsay,) with a small party of Indians, came on to take him. He, however, by some means found that they were near, and gave me his box of money and trinkets to keep safely till he called for it, and again took to the woods. Nettles came on, determined, at all events, to take him before he went back; and, in order to accomplish his design, he, with his Indians, hunted in the day time, and lay by at night at my house; and in that way they practiced for a number of days. Allen watched the motions of his pursuers, and every night after they had gone to rest, came home and got some food, and then returned to his retreat.

It was in the fall, and the weather was cold and rainy, so that he suffered extremely. Some nights he sat in my chamber till nearly daybreak, while his enemies were below; and when the time arrived, I assisted him to escape unnoticed. Nettles at length abandoned the chase, went home, and Allen, all in tatters, came in. By running in the woods his clothing had become torn into rags, so that he was in a suffering condition, almost naked. Hiokatoo gave him a blanket, and a piece of broadcloth for a pair of trousers. Allen made his trousers himself, and then built a raft, on which he went down the river to his own place at Mount Morris.

About that time he married a squaw, whose name was Sally.

The Niagara people, finding that he was at his own house, came and took him by surprise, and carried him to Niagara. Fortunately for him, it so happened that just as they arrived at the fort, a house took fire, and his keepers all left him, to save the building if possible. Allen had supposed his doom to be nearly sealed; but, finding himself at liberty, he took to his heels, left his escort to put out the fire, and ran to Tonawanda. There an Indian gave him some refreshments, and a good gun, with which he hastened on to Little Beard's Town, where

117

he found his squaw. Not daring to risk himself at that place, for fear of being given up, he made her but a short visit, and came immediately to Gardeau.

Just as he got to the top of the hill above the Gardeau Flats, he discovered a party of British soldiers and Indians in pursuit of him; and, in fact, they were so near that he was satisfied that they saw him, and concluded that it would be impossible for him to escape. The love of liberty, however, added to his natural swiftness, gave him sufficient strength to make his escape to his former castle of safety. His pursuers came immediately to my house, where they expected to have found him secreted, and under my protection. They told me where they had seen him but a few moments before, and that they were confident that it was within my power to put him into their hands.

As I was perfectly clear of having had any hand in his escape, I told them plainly that I had not seen him since he was taken to Niagara, and that I could give them no information at all respecting him. Still unsatisfied, and doubting my veracity, they advised my Indian brother to use his influence to draw from me the secret of his concealment, which they had an idea that I considered of great importance, not only to him, but to myself. I persisted in my ignorance of his situation, and finally they left me.

Although I had not seen Allen, I knew his place of security, and was well aware that, if I told them the place where he had formerly hid himself, they would have no difficulty in making him a prisoner.

He came to my house in the night, and awoke me with the greatest caution, fearing that some of his enemies might be watching to take him at a time when, and in a place where, it would be impossible for him to make his escape. I got up, and assured him that he was then safe; but that his enemies would return early in the morning, and search him out if it should be possible. Having given him some victuals, which he received thankfully, I told him to go, but to return the next night to a certain corner of the fence near my house, where he would find a quantity of meal that I would have prepared and deposited there for his use.

Early the next morning, Nettles and his company came in while I was pounding the meal for Allen, and insisted upon my giving him up. I again told them that I did not know where he was, and that I could not, neither would I, tell them anything about him. I well knew that Allen considered his life in my hands; and although it was my intention not to lie, I was fully determined to keep his situation a profound secret. They continued their labour, and examined, as they supposed, every crevice, gully, tree, and hollow log in the neighbouring woods, and at last concluded that he had left the country, gave him up for lost, and returned home.

At that time Allen lay in a secret place in the gulf, a short distance above my flats, in a hole that he accidentally found in a rock near the river. At night he came and got the meal at the corner of the fence as I had directed him, and afterward lived in the gulf two weeks. Each night he came to the pasture and milked one of my cows, without any other vessel in which to receive the milk than his hat; out of which he drank it. I supplied him with meal, but, fearing to build a fire, he was obliged to eat it raw, and wash it down with the milk. Nettles having left our neighbourhood, and Allen considering himself safe, left his little cave, and came home. I gave him his box of money and trinkets, and he went to his own house at Mount Morris.

It was generally considered, by the Indians of our tribe, that Allen was an innocent man, and that the Niagara people were persecuting him without a just cause. Little Beard, then about to go to the eastward on public business, charged his Indians not to meddle with Allen, but to let him live among them peaceably, and enjoy himself with his family and property if he could. Having the protection of the chief, he felt himself safe, and let his situation be known to the whites, from whom he suspected no harm. They, however, were more inimical than our Indians, and were easily bribed by Nettles to assist in bringing him to justice. Nettles came on, and the whites, as they had agreed, gave poor Allen up to him. He was bound, and carried to Niagara, where he was confined in prison through the winter. In the spring he was taken to Montreal or Quebec for trial, and was honourably acquitted. The crime for which he was tried was for having carried the *wampum* to the Americans, and thereby putting too sudden a stop to their war.

From the place of his trial he went directly to Philadelphia, and purchased on credit a boat-load of goods, which he brought by water to Conhocton, where he left them, and came to Mount Morris for assistance to get them brought on. The Indians readily went with horses, and brought them to his house, where he disposed of his dry goods; but not daring to let the Indians begin to drink strong liquor, for fear of the quarrels which would naturally follow, he sent his spirits to my place, where we sold them. For his goods he received ginseng roots, principally, and a few skins. Ginseng at that time was plenty, and commanded a high price. We prepared the whole that he received for the market, expecting that he would carry them to Philadelphia. In that I was disappointed; for, when he had disposed of, and got pay for all his goods, he took the ginseng and skins to Niagara, and there sold them, and came home.

Tired of dealing in goods, he planted a large field of corn on or near his own land, attended to it faithfully, and succeeded in raising a large crop, which he harvested, loaded into canoes, and carried down the river to the mouth of Allen's Creek, then called by the Indians Gin-is-a-ga, where he unloaded it, built him a house, and lived with his family.

The next season he planted corn at that place, and built a grist and saw-mill on Genesee Falls, now called Rochester.

At the time Allen built the mills, he had an old German living with him by the name of Andrews, whom he sent in a canoe down the river with his mill-irons. Allen went down at the same time; but, before they got to the mills, Allen threw the old man overboard, as it was then generally believed, for he was never seen or heard of afterward.

In the course of the season in which Allen built his mills, he became acquainted with the daughter of a white man who was moving to Niagara. She was handsome, and Allen soon got into her good graces, so that he married and took her home, to be a joint partner with Sally, the squaw, whom she had never heard of till she got home and found her in full possession; but it was too late to retrace the hasty steps she had taken, for her father had left her in the care of a tender husband, and gone on. She, however, found that she enjoyed at least an equal half of her husband's affections, and made herself contented. Her father's name I have forgotten, but hers was Lucy.

Allen was not contented with two wives, for in a short time after he had married Lucy he came up to my house, where he found a young woman who had an old husband with her. They had been on a long journey, and called at my place to recruit and rest themselves. She filled Allen's eye, and he accordingly fixed upon a plan to get her into his possession. He praised his situation, enumerated his advantages, and finally persuaded them to go home and tarry with him a few days at least, and partake of a part of his comforts. They accepted his generous invitation, and went home with him. But they had been there but two or three days, when Allen took the old gentleman out to view his flats; and as they were deliberately walking on the bank of the river, pushed him into the water. The old man, almost strangled, succeeded in getting out; but his fall and exertions had so powerful an effect upon his system that he died in two or three days, and left his young widow to the protection of his murderer. She lived with him about one year, in a state of concubinage, and then left him.

How long Allen lived at Allen's Creek I am unable to state; but soon after the young widow left him, he removed to his old place at Mount Morris, and built a house, where he made Sally—his squaw, by whom he had two daughters—a slave to Lucy, by whom he had one son; still, however, he considered Sally to be his wife. After Allen came to Mount Morris at that time, he married a girl by the name of Morilla Gregory, whose father, at the time, lived on Genesee Flats. The ceremony being over, he took her home to live in common with his other wives; but his house was too small for his family—for Sally and Lucy, conceiving that their lawful privileges would be abridged if they received a partner, united their strength, and whipped poor Morilla so cruelly that he was obliged to keep her in a small, Indian house, a short distance from his own, or lose her entirely. Morilla, before she left Mount Morris, had four children.

One of Morilla's sisters lived with Allen about a year after Morilla was married, and then quit him.

A short time after they had been living at Mount Morris, Allen prevailed upon the chiefs to give to his Indian children a tract of land two miles square, where he then resided. The chiefs gave them the land, but he so artfully contrived the conveyance that he could apply it to his own use, and by alienating his right, destroy the claim of his children.

Having secured the land in that way to himself, he sent his two Indian girls to Trenton, N.J., and his white son to Philadelphia, for the purpose of giving each of them a respectable English education.

While his children were at school, he went to Philadelphia, and sold his right to the land, which he had begged of the Indians for his children, to Robert Morris. After that, he sent for his daughters to come home, which they did.

Having disposed of the whole of his property on the Genesee River, he took his two white wives and their children, together with his effects, and removed to Delaware Town, on the River De Trench, in Upper Canada. When he left Mount Morris, Sally, his squaw, insisted upon going with him, and actually followed him, crying bitterly, and praying for his protection, some two or three miles, till he absolutely bade her leave him, or he would punish her with severity. At length finding her case hopeless, she returned to the Indians.

At the great treaty in 1797, one of Allen's daughters claimed the Mount Morris tract, which her father had sold to Robert Morris. The claim was examined, and decided against her, in favour of Morris' creditors.

He died at the Delaware Town, on the River De Trench, in the year 1814 or 1815, and left two white widows and one squaw, with a number of children, to lament his loss.

By his last will, he gave all his property to his last wife, Morilla, and her children, without providing in the least for the support of Lucy, or any of the other members of his family. Lucy, soon after his death, went with her children down the Ohio River, to receive assistance from her friends.

In the Revolutionary War, Allen was a Tory, and by that means became acquainted with our Indians, when they were in the neighbourhood of his native place, desolating the settlements on the Susquehanna. In those predatory battles he joined them, and for cruelty was not exceeded by his Indian comrades.

At one time, when he was scouting with the Indians, he entered a house very early in the morning, where he found a man, his wife, and one child, in bed. The man instantly sprang on the floor, for the purpose of defending himself and little family; but Allen dispatched him at one blow. He then cut off his head, and threw it, bleeding, into the bed with the terrified woman; took the little infant from its mother's breast, dashed its head against the jamb, and left the unhappy widow and mother, to mourn alone over her murdered family. It has been said by some, that, after he had killed the child, he opened the fire, and buried it under the coals and embers; but of that I am not certain. I have often heard him speak of that transaction with a great degree of sorrow, and as the foulest crime he had ever committed one for which I have no doubt he repented.[2]

2. "Governor Simcoe granted him three thousand acres of land, upon condition that he would build a saw-mill, a grist-mill, and a church—all but the church to be his property. He performed his part of the contract, and the title to his land was confirmed. In a few years he had his mills, a comfortable dwelling, large improvements, was a good liver, and those who knew him at that period represent him as hospitable and obliging. About the year 1806, or 1807, reverses began to overtake him. At one period he was arrested, and tried for forgery; at another, for passing counterfeit money; at another, for larceny. He was acquitted of each offense upon trial. He was obnoxious to many of his white neighbours, and it is likely that at least two of the charges against him arose out of a combination that was promoted by personal enmity. All this brought on embarrassments, which terminated in an almost entire loss of his large property. He died in 1814."—Turner's *History of the Holland Purchase.*

CHAPTER 17

# Religious Beliefs

The government of the Six Nations when they were in the ze-
nith of their prosperity and power, was an oligarchy, composed of a
mixture of elective and hereditary power; and to the skeleton of such
a government the remnant of the race still adhere. Their government
was administered by chiefs—each tribe having two; one of whom was
hereditary, and the other elective; the term of whose office was during good behaviour, and might be removed for any real or supposed
sufficient cause, which, however, was seldom put in execution. The
elective *sachem* was the military chieftain, whose duty it was, to attend
to all the military concerns of the tribe, and command the warriors
in battle. They were both members of the general council of the confederacy, as well as of the national council, which met as often as necessity required, and settled all questions, involving matters in which
their own nation only had an interest; but the general council of the
confederacy met but once a year, except in cases of emergency.

It then met at Onondaga, being the headquarters of the most cen-
tral nation, where all great questions of general interest, such as peace
and war—the concerns of tributary nations, and all negotiations with
the French and English were debated, deliberated upon, and decided.
All decisions made by the chiefs of a tribe, which affected the members
of that tribe only—all decisions of the national council, solely relative
to the affairs of that nation, (a majority of chiefs concurring,)[1]and all
decisions of the general council of the confederacy, were laws and de-
crees from which there was no appeal. There is also a class of counsel-
lors in the several tribes, who have great influence over, but no direct

---

1. The author has fallen into an error in this particular. It was a fundamental law of
the confederacy, and also of each nation, that the chiefs "must be of one mind;" that
is, unanimous.

123

voice in the decision of any question. [2]

Perhaps no people are more exact observers of religious duties, than those Indians among the Senecas who are denominated Pagans, in contradistinction from those, who, having renounced some of their former superstitious notions, have obtained the name of Christians. The traditionary faith of their fathers, having been orally trans- mitted to them from time immemorial, is implicitly believed, scrupulously adhered to, and rigidly practiced. They are agreed in their sentiments—are all of one order; individual and public good, especially among themselves, being the great motive which excites them to attend to those moral virtues that are directed and explained by all their rules, and in all their ceremonies.

Many years have elapsed since the introduction of Christian missionaries among them, whom they have heard, and very generally understand the purport of the message they were sent to deliver. They say that it is highly probable that Jesus Christ came into the world in

---

2. "At the institution of the league fifty permanent *sachemships* were created, with appropriate names; and in the *sachems* who held these titles were rested the supreme power of the confederacy. To secure order in the succession, and to determine the individuals entitled, the *sachemships* were made hereditary, under. limited and peculiar laws of descent. The *sachems* themselves were equal in rank and authority, and instead of holding separate territorial jurisdictions, their powers were joint and coextensive with the league. As a safeguard against contention and fraud, such *sachem* was "raised up," and invested with his title, by a council of all the *sachems*, with suitable forms and ceremonies. Until this ceremony of confirmation or investiture, no one could become a ruler. He received, when raised up, the name of the *sachemship* itself, as in the case of the titles of nobility, and so also did his successors, from generation to generation. The *sachemships* were distributed unequally between the five nations. Nine of them were assigned to the Mohawk nation, nine to the Oneida, fourteen to the Onondaga, ten to the Cayuga, and eight to the Seneca. The *sachems*, united, formed the council of the League—the ruling body in whom resided the executive, legislative, and judicial authority.

It thus appears that the government of the Iroquois was an oligarchy, taking the term, at least, in the literal sense, "the rule of the few;" and while more system is observable in this, than in the oligarchies of antiquity, it seems, also, better calculated in its framework to resist political changes. . . . Next to the *sachems*, in position, stood the chiefs—an inferior class of rulers, the very existence of whose office was an anomaly in the oligarchy of the Iroquois. The office of chief was made elective, and the reward of merit; but without any power of descent, the title terminating with the individual. . . . . . After their election they were raised up by a council of the nation; but a ratification by the general council of the *sachems* was necessary to complete the investiture. The powers and duties of the sachems and chiefs were entirely of a civil character, and confined by their organic laws to the affairs of peace."—
*League of the Iroquois.*

old times, to establish a religion that would promote the happiness of the white people on the other side of the great water, (meaning the sea), and that he died for the sins of his people, as the missionaries have informed them. But, they say that Jesus Christ had nothing to do with them; and that the Christian religion was not designed for their benefit; but rather, should they embrace it, they are confident it would make them worse, and consequently do them an injury.

They say also, that the Great Good Spirit gave them their religion; and that it is better adapted to their circumstances, situation, and habits, and to the promotion of their present comfort, and ultimate happiness, than any system that ever has or can be devised. They, however, believe that the Christian religion is better calculated for the good of white people than theirs is, and wonder that those who have embraced it, do not attend more strictly to its precepts, and feel more engaged for its support and diffusion among themselves. At the present time, they are opposed to preachers or schoolmasters being sent or coming among them, and appear determined by all means to adhere to their ancient customs.

They believe in a Great Good Spirit, whom they call in the Seneca language *Nau-wah-ne-u*,[3] as the creator of the world, and of every good thing; that he made men, and all inoffensive animals; that he supplies men with all the comforts of life; and that he is particularly partial to the Indians, who, they say, are his peculiar people. They also believe that he is pleased in giving them (the Indians) good gifts; and that he is highly gratified with their good conduct, that he abhors their vices, and that he is willing to punish them for their bad conduct, not only in this world but in a future state of existence. His residence, they suppose, lies at a great distance from them, in a country that is perfectly pleasant, where plenty abounds, even to profusion. That there the soil is completely fertile, and the seasons so mild that the corn never fails to be good—that the deer, elk, buffalo, turkeys, and other useful animals, are numerous, and that the forests are well calculated to facilitate their hunting them with success—that the streams are pure, and abound with fish; and nothing is wanting, to render fruition complete. Over this territory they say Nauwahneu presides as an all-powerful king; and that without counsel he admits to his pleasures all whom he considers to be worthy of enjoying so great a state of blessedness. To this Being they address prayers, offer sacrifices, give thanks for favours, and perform many acts of devotion and reverence.

3. *Há-wen-né-yu.*

125

They likewise believe that Nauwahneu has a brother that is less powerful than himself, and who is opposed to him, and every one that is or wishes to be good; that this Bad Spirit[4] made all evil things, snakes, wolves, catamounts, and all other poisonous or noxious animals and beasts of prey, except the bear, which, on the account of the excellence of its meat for food, and skin for clothing, they say was made by Nauwahneu. Besides all this, they say he makes and sends them their diseases, bad weather, and bad crops; and that he makes and supports witches. He owns a large country adjoining that of his brother, with whom he is continually at variance. His fields are unproductive; thick clouds intercept the rays of the sun, and consequently destructive frosts are frequent; game is very scarce, and not easily taken; ravenous beasts are numerous; reptiles of every poisoned tooth lie in the path of the traveller; the streams are muddy; and hunger, nakedness, and general misery, are severely felt by those who unfortunately become his tenants.

He takes pleasure in afflicting the Indians here, and, after their death, receives all those into his dreary dominions who, in their lifetime have been so vile as to be rejected by Nauwahneu, under whose eye they are continued in an uncomfortable state forever. To this source of evil they offer some oblations, to abate his vengeance, and render him propitious. They, however, believe him to be, in a degree, under subjection to his brother, and incapable of executing his plans only by his high permission. Public religious duties are attended to in the celebration of particular festivals and sacrifices, which are observed with circumspection, and attended with decorum. In each year they have five feasts,[5] or stated times for assembling in their tribes, and giving thanks to Nauwahneu, for the blessings which they have received from his kind, liberal, and provident hand; and also to converse upon the best means of meriting a continuance of his favours.

---

4. *Ha-ne-go-até-geh*, the "Evil-minded."
5. "Six regular festivals, or 'thanksgivings,' were observed by the Iroquois. The first in the order of time was the Maple festival. This was a return of thanks to the maple itself, for yielding its sweet waters. Next was the Planting festival, designed chiefly as an invocation of the Great Spirit to bless the seed. Third came the Strawberry festival, instituted as a thanksgiving for the first fruits of the earth. The fourth was the Green Corn festival, designed as a thanksgiving acknowledgement for the ripening of the corn, beans, and squashes. Next was celebrated the Harvest festival, instituted as a general thanksgiving to 'our supporters,' after the gathering of the harvest. Last in the enumeration is placed the New Year's festival, the great jubilee of the Iroquois, at which the white dog was sacrificed."—*League of the Iroquois*.

The first, of these feasts is immediately after they have finished sugaring, at which time they give thanks for the favourable weather and great quantity of sap they have had, and for the sugar that they have been allowed to make for the benefit of their families. At this, as at all the succeeding feasts, the chiefs arise singly, and address the audience in a kind of exhortation, in which they express their own thankfulness, urge the necessity and propriety of general gratitude, and point out the course which ought to be pursued by each individual, in order that Nauwahneu may continue to bless them, and that the evil spirit may be defeated.

On these occasions the chiefs describe a perfectly straight line, half an inch wide, and perhaps ten miles long, which they direct their people to travel upon, by placing one foot before the other, with the heel of one foot on the toe of the other; and so on till they arrive at the end. The meaning of which is, that they must not turn aside to the right hand or to the left into the paths of vice; but keep straight ahead in the way of well-doing, that will lead them to the paradise of Nauwahneu.

The second feast is after planting; when they render thanks for the pleasantness of the season; for the good time they have had for preparing their ground and planting their corn; and are instructed by their chiefs by what means to merit a good harvest.

When the green corn becomes fit for use, they hold their third or green corn feast. Their fourth is celebrated after corn harvest; and the fifth at the close of their year, and is always celebrated at the time of the old moon in the last of January or first of February. This last deserves particular description.

The Indians having returned from hunting, and having brought in all the venison and skins that they have taken, a committee is appointed, consisting of from ten to twenty active men, to superintend the festivities of the great sacrifice and thanksgiving that is to be immediately celebrated. This being done, preparations are made at the council-house, or place of meeting, for the reception and accommodation of the whole tribe; and then the ceremonies are commenced; and the whole is conducted with a great degree of order and harmony, under the direction of the committee.

Two white dogs, without spot or blemish, are selected, (if such can be found, and if not, two that have the fewest spots,) from those belonging to the tribe, and killed near the door of the council-house, by being strangled. A wound on the animal, or an effusion of blood, would spoil the victim, and render the sacrifice useless. The dogs are then painted red on their faces, edges of their ears, and on various parts of their bodies, and are curiously decorated with ribbons of different colours, and fine feathers, which are tied and fastened on in such a manner as to make the most elegant appearance. They are then hung on a post near the door of the council-house, at the height of twenty feet from the ground. The practice of sacrificing two dogs was formerly strictly adhered to, but at present they sacrifice only one. This being done, the frolic is commenced by those who are present, while the committee run through the tribe, and hurry the people to assemble, by knocking on their houses.

At this time the committee are naked—wearing only a breech-clout—and each carries a paddle, with which he takes up ashes, and scatters them about the house in every direction. In the course of the ceremonies, all the fire is extinguished in every hut throughout the tribe, and new fire, struck from the flint on each hearth, is kindled, after having removed the whole of the ashes, old coals, etc. Having done this, and discharged one or two guns, they go on; and in this manner they proceed till they have visited every house in the tribe. This finishes the business of the first day.

On the second day, the committee dance, go through the town with bearskin on their legs; and at every time they start they fire a gun. They also beg through the tribe, each carrying a basket in which to receive whatever may be bestowed. The alms consist of Indian to-bacco, and other articles that are used for incense or sacrifice. Each manager, at this time, carries a dried tortoise or turtle shell, containing a few beans, which he frequently rubs on the walls of the houses, both inside and out. This kind of manoeuvring by the committee continues two or three days, during which time the people at the council-house recreate themselves by dancing.

On the fourth or fifth day, the committee make false faces of the husks, in which they run about, making a frightful but ludicrous appearance. In this dress, still wearing the bearskin, they run to the council-house, smearing themselves with dirt, and bedaub everyone who refuses to contribute something toward filling the basket of incense, which they continue to carry, soliciting alms. During all this time, they collect the Evil Spirit, or drive it off entirely, for the present, and also concentrate within themselves all the sins of their tribe, however numerous or heinous.

On the eighth or ninth day, the committee having received all their sins, as before observed, into their own bodies, they take down the dogs and after having transfused the whole of them into one of their own number, he, by a peculiar sleight of hand, or kind of magic, works them all out of himself into the dogs. The dogs, thus loaded with all the sins of the people, are placed upon a pile of wood, that is directly set on fire. Here they are burned, together with the sins with which they were loaded, surrounded by the multitude, who throw incense of tobacco, or the like, into the fire, the scent of which, they say, goes up to Nauwahneu, to whom it is pleasant and acceptable.[6]

This feast formerly continued nine days, but at present it is not usually held more than from five to seven, although until within a few years nine days were strictly observed; and during that time the chiefs review the national affairs of the year past; agree upon the best plan to be pursued through the next year, and attend to all internal regulations.

On the last day, the whole company partake of a dinner in common, consisting of meat, corn, and beans, boiled together in large kettles, and stirred till the whole is comletely mixed and soft. This mess is devoured without much ceremony. Some eat with a spoon,

---

6. "On the morning of the fifth day, soon after dawn, the white dog was burned on an altar of wood, erected by the "keepers of the faith," near the council-house. It is difficult, from outward observation, to draw forth the true intent with which the dog was burned. The obscurity with which the object was veiled has led to various conjectures. Among other things, it has been pronounced a sacrifice for sin. In the religious system of the Iroquois there is no recognition of the doctrine of atonement for sin, or of the absolution or forgiveness of sins. Upon this whole subject their system is silent. An act once done, was registered beyond the power of change. The greatest advance upon this point of faith was, the belief that good deeds cancelled the evil, thus placing heaven, through good works, within the reach of all. The notion that this was an expiation for sin and thus refuted by their system of theology itself. The other idea, that the sins of the people, by some mystic process, were transferred to the dog, and by him thus borne away, on the principle of the scapegoat of the Hebrews, is also without any foundation in truth. The burning of the dog had not the slightest connection with the sin of the people. On the contrary, the simple idea of the sacrifice was, to send up the spirit of the dog as a messenger to the Great Spirit, to announce their continued fidelity to his service, and, also, to convey to him united thanks for the blessings of the year. The fidelity of the dog, the companion of the Indian, as a hunter, was emblematical of their fidelity. No messenger so trusty could be found, to bear their petitions to the Master of Life. The Iroquois believed that the Great Spirit made a covenant with their fathers, to the effect that, when they should send up to him the spirit of a dog, of a spotless white, he would receive it as a pledge of their adherence to his worship, and his ears would thus be opened in a special degree to their petitions."—*League of the Iroquois.*

by dipping out of the kettles; others serve themselves in small dippers; some in one way, and some in another, till the whole is consumed. After this, they perform the war-dance, the peace-dance, and smoke the pipe of peace; and then, free from iniquity, each repairs to his place of abode, prepared to commence a new year. In this feast, temperance is observed, and commonly order prevails in a greater degree than would naturally be expected.

They are fond of the company of spectators, who are disposed to be decent, and treat them politely in their way; but having been frequently imposed upon by the whites, they treat them generally with indifference

Even their dances appear to be religious rites, especially their war and peace dances. The war-dance is said to have originated about the time that the Six Nations, or Northern Indians, commenced the old war with the Cherokees and other southern Indian nations, about one hundred years ago.

When a tribe, or a number of tribes, of the Six Nations had assembled for the purpose of going to battle with their enemies, the chiefs sang this song, and accompanied the music with dancing, and gestures that corresponded with the sentiments expressed, as a kind of stimulant to increase their courage and anxiety, to march forward to the place of carnage.

Those days having passed away, the Indians at this day sing the "war-song," to commemorate the achievements of their fathers, and as a kind of amusement, When they perform it, they arm themselves with a war-club, tomahawk, and knife, and commence singing with a firm voice, and a stern, resolute countenance; but before they get through, they exhibit in their features and actions the most shocking appearance of anger, fury, and vengeance, that can be imagined. No exhibition of the kind can be more terrifying to a stranger.

The peace-dance is performed to a tune without words, by both sexes. The Indians stand erect, in one place, and strike the floor with the heel and toes of one foot, and then of the other, (the heels and toes all the while nearly level,) without changing their position in the least. The squaws at the same time perform it, by keeping the feet close together, and, without raising them from the ground, move a short distance to the right, and then to left, by first moving their toes, and then their heels. This dance is beautiful, and is generally attended with decency

No people on earth *appear* to be so strictly moral—in conformity to their laws, and customs—as the North American Indians generally, in their intercourse between the sexes. The several nations have different forms of approaching to courtship and marriage, which, however, are all very similar—most of the tribes tolerate and practice polygamy and divorce; some, however, do not. Among the Senecas, both are tolerated, and practiced to some extent.

For neither marriage nor divorce is there any particular form or ceremony, other than when an Indian sees a squaw whom he fancies, he sends a present to her mother or parents, who, on receiving it, consult with his parents, his friends, and each other, on the propriety and expediency of the proposed connection. If it is not agreeable, the present is returned; but if it is, the lover is informed of his good fortune, and immediately goes to live with her, or takes her to a hut of his own preparing.[7]

---

7. "Marriage was not founded upon the affections, which constitute the only legitimate basis of this relation in civilized society, but was regulated exclusively as a matter of physical necessity. It was not even a contract between the parties to be married; but substantially between their mothers, acting oftentimes under the suggestions of the matrons and wise men of the tribes to which the parties respectively belonged. .

". . . . When the mother considered her son of a suitable age for marriage, she looked about her for a maiden, whom, from report or acquaintance, she judged would accord with him in disposition and temperament. A negotiation between the mothers ensued, and a conclusion was speedily reached. Sometimes the near relatives, and the elderly persons of the tribes to which each belonged, were consulted; but their opinions were of no avail, independently of the wishes of the mothers themselves. Not the least singular feature of the transaction was the entire ignorance in which the parties remained of the pending negotiation; the first intimation they received being the announcement of their marriage, without, perhaps, ever having known or seen each other. Remonstrance or objection on their part was never attempted; they received each other as the gift of their parents. As obedience to them in all their requirements was inculcated as a paramount duty, and disobedience was followed by disownment, the operative force of custom, in addition to these motives, was sufficient to secure acquiescence. The Indian father never troubled himself concerning the marriage of his children. To interfere would have been an invasion of female immunities; and these, whatever they were, were as sacredly regarded by him, as he was inflexible in enforcing for his own.

"From the very nature of the marriage institution among the Iroquois, it follows that the passion of love was entirely unknown among them. Affection after marriage would naturally spring up between the parties, from association, from habit, and from mutual dependence; but of that marvellous passion which originates in a higher development of the powers of the human heart, and is founded upon a cultivation of the affections between the sexes, they were entirely ignorant. In their temperaments they were below this passion in its (continued next page),

131

If a difficulty of importance arises between a married couple, they agree to separate. They divide their property and children; the squaw takes the girls, the Indian the boys, and both are at liberty to marry again.

From all history and tradition, it would appear that neither seduction, prostitution, nor rape, was known in the calendar of crimes of this rude savage race, until the females were contaminated by the embrace of civilized man. And it is a remarkable fact, that, among the great number of women and girls who have been taken prisoners by the Indians during the last two centuries, although they have often been tomahawked and scalped, their bodies ripped open while alive, and otherwise barbarously tortured, not a single instance is on record, or has ever found currency in the great stock of gossip and story which civilized society is so prone to circulate, that a female prisoner has ever been ill-treated, abused, or her modesty insulted, by an Indian, with reference to her sex. This universal trait in the Indian character cannot be wholly, if in the least, attributed to the cold temperament of their constitutions—the paucity of their animal functions, or want of natural propensities—for polygamy is not only tolerated but extensively indulged in, among nearly all the North American tribes. Of this we have the most abundant proof, not relying solely on the testimony of Mrs. Jemison, who states that it was tolerated and practiced in the Seneca nation, but on the statements of all writers on that subject, and of all travellers and sojourners in the Indian country.

Major Marston, commanding officer at the U. S. Fort Armstrong, in the North-western Territory, in 1820, in an official report to our government, relative to the condition, customs, religion, etc. of the various tribes of the North-western Indians, states, that "many of these Indians have two or three wives; the greatest number that I have known any man to have at one time, was five. When an Indian wants more than one wife, he generally prefers that they be sisters, as they are more likely to agree, and live together in harmony. A man of fifty

---

simplest forms. Attachments between individuals, or the cultivation of each other's affections before marriage, was entirely unknown; so also were promises of marriage. The fact that individuals were united in this relation, without their knowledge or consent, and perhaps without even a previous acquaintance, illustrates and confirms this position. This invasion of the romances of the novelist, and of the conceits of the poet, upon the attachments which sprang up in the bosom of Indian society, may, perhaps, divest the mind of some pleasing impressions; but these are entirely inconsistent with the marriage institution, as it existed among them, and with the facts of their social history."—*League of the Iroquois.*

or sixty years old, who has two or three wives, will frequently marry a girl of sixteen."

On the other hand, this abstemiousness cannot be attributed to the dictates of moral virtue, as that would be in direct opposition to all their other traits of character. And, again, no society or race of men exists, so purely moral, but that, if there was any crime within their power to perpetrate, to which they were prompted by their passions, some one or more would be guilty of committing it, if restrained by moral virtue only.

Therefore we are driven to the conclusion, that the young warrior has been taught and trained up from his infancy, to subdue this passion; and to effect that object, he has been operated upon by some direful, superstitious awe, and appalling fear of the consequences of the violation of female chastity; and, with the same anathema held to his view, taught to avoid temptation, by demeaning himself perfectly uninquisitive and modest, in the presence of females, and especially female prisoners. It is not supposed, however, that great exertions are made at the present day, to instil those prejudices, if I may be allowed so to apply the word, into the Indian youth, for those dicta have been so long promulgated, and obedience thereto so rigidly enforced, through so many generations that they have become an inborn characteristic of the race.

We can easily perceive the policy of the ancient founders of this precautionary branch of savage education, and it is worthy of the paternity of a Solon. By this precaution, jealousy, feuds, strife; and bloodshed, are avoided among the warriors, while they are out on their predatory excursions, stealthily seizing prisoners, scalps, or plunder by night, or warily and noiselessly winding their course through the forest by day.

# CHAPTER 18[1]

# Life of Mary Continued

More than eighteen years have elapsed, (as at time of first publication), since Mary Jemison related the preceding narrative of her life, and most of its appendages, to our deceased friend, the author of the first edition; during which period many important incidents have transpired, and material changes taken place involving the destiny of the principal subject of this memoir, her family and friends, although none very remarkable or unexpected.

Mary Jemison continued to reside on her flats, plant, hoe, and harvest her corn, beans, squashes, etc., annually, in the same routine of laborious activity and undisturbed tranquillity, which she had always pursued and enjoyed, in times of peace in the nation, and concord in her family. But the evening of her eventful life was not suffered thus smoothly to pass away. The Senecas having sold all their reservations on the Genesee River in 1825, and given possession to the whites soon after, they removed with their families to Tonawanda, Buffalo Crock, and Cattaraugus reservations, leaving Mrs. Jemison, her daughters, and their husbands, on her two square miles, surrounded by the whites in every direction. Thus situated, she and her children grew as discontented and uneasy, as Alexander Selkirk was on the Island of Juan Fernandez.

They determined to leave their solitary and isolated abode among the whites, and again join their tribe, mix in the society, and partake of the joys and the sorrows of their kindred and friends. With this in view, Mrs. Jemison sold her annuity of three hundred dollars *per annum*, or rather, received of the obligors a commutation therefore, in ready money. She likewise sold her remaining two square miles of

---

1. This chapter was written by Ebenezer Mix, Esqr.

SHOWING HER HOUSE AND MODERN IMPROVEMENTS.

land, including her "flats," to Messrs. Henry B. Gibson and Jellis Clute. In the summer of 1831, she removed to Buffalo Creek reservation, where she purchased the Indian possessory right to a good farm on the Buffalo Flats, on which she resided in a state of peace and quietude, until the time of her decease.

Mrs. Jemison's good traits of character were not wholly of the negative kind; she exhibited a rare example of unostentatious charity and true benevolence. She appeared to take pleasure and self-satisfaction in relieving the distress, and supplying the wants of her fellow-creatures, whether white or red; anything she possessed, however much labour it might have cost her, was freely given, when she thought the necessities of others required it. It would redound much to the honour of the Christian religion, if some of its members would pattern, in some measures, after the pagan woman, in practicing this most exalted of Christian virtues, charity, in feelings as well as in actions.

The bodily infirmities of old age gradually increased in Mrs. Jemison, and enervated her frame; yet she retained her reason and mental faculties to an uncommon extent, for a person of her age; and her society was not only endurable, but rendered highly interesting and desirable, by her natural exuberant flow of animal spirits and good nature. In the summer of 1833, she, in a peaceable and friendly manner, seceded from the pagan party of her nation, and joined the Christian party, having in her own view, and to the satisfaction of her spiritual instructor, the Rev. Asher Wright, missionary at that station, repudiated paganism, and embraced the Christian religion.

In the autumn succeeding, she was attacked by disease for almost the first time in her protracted pilgrimage, and dropped away suddenly from the scenes of this life, on the 19th day of September, 1833. at her own dwelling on the Buffalo Creek reservation, aged about ninety-one years. Her funeral was conducted after the manner, and with the usual ceremonies practiced at Christian burials; and was attended by a large concourse of people. A marble slab now marks the spot where her earthly remains rest, in the graveyard near the Seneca Mission church, with the following inscription:

In
Memory of
THE WHITE WOMAN,
MARY JEMISON,
Daughter of

THOMAS JEMISON & JANE IRWIN,
Born on the ocean, between Ireland and Phila., in 1742 or 3.
Taken captive at Marsh Creek, Pa. in 1755 carried down the Ohio,
Adopted into an Indian family. In 1759 removed to Genesee River.
Was naturalized in 1817. Removed to this place in 1831.
And having survived two husbands and five children,
leaving three still alive;
She Died Sept 19th 1833 aged about ninety-one years,
Having a few weeks before expressed a hope of pardon through
JESUS CHRIST,
"The counsel of the Lord that shall stand."

Mrs. Jemison's three children, Betsey, Nancy, and Polly, who survived her, all lived respected, and died regretted, at their several places of residence on the Seneca reservations, in the short space of three months, in the autumn of 1839, aged, respectively, sixty-nine, sixty-three, and fifty-eight years, leaving a large number of children and grandchildren to lament their loss.

Jacob Jemison, the grandson of Mrs. Jemison, mentioned by her in Chapter 10, as having received a liberal education, and having commenced the study of medicine, passed through a regular course of medical studies, with great success, and was appointed an assistant surgeon in the United States Navy; in which capacity he sustained an excellent moral, social, and professional character, which requires no stronger confirmation, than the laconic eulogium pronounced by Captain E., the commander of the vessel on board of which he performed duty. Captain E., being asked by a gentleman who had known Jemison when a boy, how he sustained the character of his situation, promptly replied: "There is no person on board the ship so generally esteemed as Mr. Jemison, nor a better surgeon in the navy." Doctor Jemison died five or six years ago, (as at time of first publication), on board his ship in the Mediterranean squadron, when about forty years of age.

Several of the grandchildren of Mrs. Jemison, now living, (as at time of first publication), are highly respected in their nation; while their talents and moral standing are duly appreciated, and their civilities reciprocated among the whites. They have acquired the use of the English language sufficiently to speak it fluently, and have adopted the dress, habits, and manners of civilized society. Her grandchildren and great-grandchildren arc numerous: they reside on the remaining

Seneca reservations in this state, at present; but will, undoubtedly, ere long, take their departure from the land of their fathers, and assume important positions in legislative and judicial stations in the now Indian territory west of the Mississippi.[2]

---

2. "The author, in his boyhood, has often seen the 'White Woman,' as she was uniformly called by the early settlers; and remembers well the general esteem in which she was held. Notwithstanding she had one son who was a terror to Indians as well as to the early white settlers, she has left many descendants who are not unworthy of her good name. Jacob Jemison, a grandson of hers, received a liberal education, passed through a course of medical studies, and was appointed assistant surgeon in the United States Navy. He died on board of his ship in the Mediterranean."— Turner's *Hist. of the Holland Purchase.*

CHAPTER 19

# The Ultimate Extinction of
# the Red Race

History and tradition alike inform us that the Mohawks, the Oneidas, the Cayugas, and the Senecas, had, from time immemorial, formed
themselves into a great confederacy, strictly adhering to an offensive
and defensive alliance. They occupied, for their dwelling grounds, a
wide-spread territory, extending from near the banks of the Hudson
to the shores of Lake Erie, and from the mouth of the Alleghany to
the confines of the St. Lawrence. This tract comprises a greater body
of more fertile land, combined with a temperate and healthy climate,
great facilities of water communication—not only within the territory, but extending from it in all directions—with extensive hunting grounds and fisheries, than any other tract of the same extent in
North America.

This territory is admirably adapted to the occupation of a roving
and migratory people, who depend more on the chase and on the
spontaneous productions of nature for sustenance, than on agriculture
and the regular productions of labour. Beside this vast domain for a
residence, they claimed an exclusive right to all that region of country
between the Ohio River and Lake Erie, (now the State of Ohio,) for
a spacious hunting ground; and the martial prowess of that mighty
confederacy enabled them promptly to repel any intrusion from other
tribes. They were indeed a mighty people—whose forces could be
seen, and whose power could be felt, and often was felt, from the
banks of the St. Lawrence to the Gulf of Mexico. and from the tides
of the Hudson to the banks of the Mississippi. Until the year 1712,
this people were called by the English "The Five Nations," or "The
Confederates;" by the French, "The Iroquois;" by the Dutch, "The

Maquas;" and by themselves "The Mingoes."[1]

During that year, the Tuscaroras, whose habitation had been in the west part of North Carolina, after some disturbances with the whites in that region, evacuated their possessions in that colony, removed to Western New York, and were adopted by the Mingoes as a sixth nation. They lived between the Oneidas and Onondagas, on lands assigned them for a residence by the former; after which, the English usually denominated the confederates "The Six Nations."[2]

In 1784, soon after peace had been ratified between the United States and Great Britain, a treaty of peace and amnesty was concluded between the United States and the Six Nations, in which their territorial limits were defined; to wit, they were to possess all the State of New York west of what was called the "Property Line," with the exception of two reservations—one of six miles square, including Fort Oswego; and the other, along the Niagara River, about thirty-five miles long and four miles wide, including forts Niagara and Schlosser, and the Portage road from Lake Ontario to Lake Erie. The Property Line here referred to was a line commencing at the north-east corner of Pennsylvania, and running in its general course a little east of north, crossing the Mohawk River, at or near the place where the division line of the counties of Herkimer and Oneida now crosses the same.

They were likewise to retain a part of Pennsylvania, but were required to cede to the United States their extensive hunting-grounds north of the Ohio, which met with violent opposition from many of the Indian chiefs and orators, but was finally acquiesced in by the council. It was on this occasion that the celebrated Red Jacket, then a youth, opened the flood-gates of his eloquence, and poured forth its magic powers, to sustain the then gradually declining, yet still lofty elevation of his people; and to check the encroachments of the whites on their territorial demesnes, which his prophetic mind clearly saw would, at no distant day, if not effectually opposed, prostrate their empire, and eradicate their race as a distinct people.

---

1. This is an error of the author. The Iroquois never called themselves the Mingoes, but always the *Ho-dé-no-san-nee*, or "The People of the Long House." They likened their confederacy to a "long house."

2. The names of the several nations, in the Seneca dialect, are as follows:—*1*. Mohawk Nation—Gä-ne-á-ga-o-nó: or, People, Possessors of the Flint. *2*. Onondaga Nation—*O-nun-dä-ga-o-nó*; or, People on the Hills. *3*. Seneca Nation—*Nun-dá-wä-o-nó*; or, Great Hill People. *4*. Oneida Nation—*O-ná-yote-kä-o-nó*; or, Granite People. *5*. Cayuga Nation—*Gwe-ú-gwch-o-nó;* or, People at the Mucky Land. *6*. Tuscarora Nation—*Dus-gào-weh-o-nó*: or, Shirt-Wearing People.

At different periods, from that time to the present, the several nations have ceded large portions of their lands to this state, and to persons holding the pre-emption right under the government; out of which, in most cases, they retained for themselves small reservations. In 1797, the last great sale was made by the Senecas to Robert Morris, being the extreme western part of the state—reducing the once extensive possessions of the Mingoes to a few small, detached reservations. The Senecas in this sale reserved the following tracts: the Cannewagus, Bigtree, Little Beard's, Squawkie Hill, Gardeau, and Caneadea, all lying on the Genesee River; the Oil Spring, Alleghany, Cattaraugus, Buffalo Creek, Tonawanda and Tuscarora reservations; containing in the whole about three hundred and thirty-seven square miles. The Tuscaroras had a donation from the Holland Land Company, of two square miles; and in 1804 they purchased of the same company 4,329 acres, for which they paid $13,752, in cash.

In 1825 the Senecas held a council, at which they sold and ceded to the persons claiming the pre-emption right to the same, all their reservations on the Genesee River, (the Gardeau reservation excepted, that being a special concern,) the Oil Spring reservation, and portions of the Cattaraugus, Buffalo Creek, and Tonawanda reservations; leaving less than one hundred and ninety square miles in Alleghany, Cattaraugus, Buffalo Creek, Tonawanda, and Tuscarora reservations.

In 1838, another treaty was held by the Senecas and Tuscaroras, at which the Senecas, (or a portion of their chiefs,) and the Tuscaroras, agreed to sell to the pre-emption right owners, called the Ogden Land Company, the residue of their reservations in western New York, and emigrate, within five years, to other lands, which they were to receive in exchange, lying in the Indian territory west of the Mississippi; since which, a violent warfare has been carried on, not only orally, but through periodicals and pamphlets, using petitions, memorials, and remonstrances in the United States government, for their heavy artillery, by a portion of the Senecas, (and probably a majority,) a few restless spirits among the whites, who always hang around the borders of Indian settlements, and the New York, Pennsylvania, and Maryland Quakers, on the one hand; who insist that, although the grossest bribery and corruption has been resorted to, the treaty has not been excited in council, according to the usages and customs of the Indians, nor has it been confirmed according to the laws of the United States; while on the other hand, the Ogden Land Company, their retainers, and a portion of the Senecas, backed by another class of worthless whites, insist that the treaty has been formally executed by all the parties, and that as a few bribes have been a distributed as is usual on such occasions.

If the only object of the nullifiers was to procure for the Indians an equivalent for their trouble and privations, in making exchange of lands, their proceedings might be justifiable; but they insist that the poor Indians shall not emigrate. It certainly cannot be of any great importance to the individuals of this remnant of the race, whether they are removed by the government, or whether they remain where they now are; provided, that in adopting either course, they do it willingly and cheerfully; and it cannot be doubted but that, if they had been left to the unbiased volition of their own minds, the Senecas, as a body, would have accepted with joy, the proposition of the government for their removal.

The Indians should be honestly and honourably dealt with, and their rights should be guarded with vigilance, and protected with firmness and effect; but as the United States government has adopted the policy of inducing all the Indians, within the territory of the several states, to leave their present abode, and retire, with the aid, and under the fostering care and protection of that government, to a country peculiarly adapted to their wants, habits, and mode of life, where no state jurisdiction can ever interfere with their laws, customs, and peculiarities, it is the duty of the citizens to assist the government in carrying its measures into effect, as far as they can do so, honestly and honourably; or at least, to remain neutral in relation thereto, and not undertake to thwart the measures of government, and at the same time render the pretended objects of their care more miserable than they otherwise would be; or we will venture to predict, that, notwithstanding the most vigorous exertions of *such* philanthropists to the contrary, the time is not far distant, when the Genius of the Empire State will behold the last of the Iroquois wending his way toward the setting sun.

# Concluding Note From "League of the Iroquois"

The future destiny of the Indian upon this continent is a subject of no ordinary interest. If the fact that he cannot be saved in his native state needed any proof beyond the experience of the past, it could be demonstrated from the nature of things. Our primitive inhabitants are environed with civilized life, the baleful and disastrous influence of which, when brought in contact with Indian life, is wholly irresistible. Civilization is aggressive as well as progressive—a positive state of society, attacking obstacle, overwhelming every lesser agency, and searching out and filling up every crevice, both in the moral and physical world; while Indian life is an unarmed condition, a negative state, without inherent vitality, and without powers of resistance.

The institutions of the red man fix him to the soil with a fragile and precarious tenure; while those of civilized man, in his highest estate, enable him to seize it with a grasp which defies displacement. To uproot a race at the meridian of its intellectual power, is next to impossible; but the expulsion of a contiguous one, in a state of primitive rudeness, is comparatively easy, if not an absolute necessity. The manifest destiny of the Indian, if left to himself, calls up the question of his reclamation, certainly, in itself, a more interesting, and far more important subject than any which have before been considered.

All the Indian races now dwelling within the Republic have fallen under its jurisdiction; thus casting upon the government a vast responsibility, as the administrator of their affairs, and a solemn trust, as the guardian of their future welfare. Should the system of tutelage and supervision adopted by the national government find its highest aim and ultimate object in the adjustment of their present difficulties from day to day, or should it look beyond and above these temporary

143

considerations, toward their final elevation to the rights and privileges of American citizens? This is certainly a grave question, and if the latter enterprise itself be feasible, it should be prosecuted with a zeal and energy as earnest and untiring as its importance demands.

During the period within which this question will be solved, the American people cannot remain indifferent and passive spectators, and avoid responsibility; for while the government is chiefly accountable for the administration of their civil affairs, those of a moral and religious character, which, at least, are not less important, appeal to the enlightened benevolence of the public at large.

Whether a portion of the Indian family may yet be reclaimed and civilized, and thus saved eventually from the fate which has already befallen so many of our aboriginal races, will furnish the theme for a few concluding reflections. What is true of the Iroquois, in a general can be predicted of any other portion of our primitive inhabitants. For this reason, the facts relied upon to establish the hypothesis that the Indian can be permanently reclaimed and civilized, will be drawn exclusively from the social history of the former.

There are now, (as at time of first publication), about four thousand Iroquois living in the state of New York. Having for many years been surrounded by civilization, and shut in from all intercourse with the ruder tribes of the wilderness, they have not only lost their native fierceness, but have become quite tractable and humane. In addition to this, the agricultural pursuits into which they have gradually become initiated, have introduced new modes of life, and awakened new aspirations, until a change, in itself scarcely perceptible to the casual observer, but in reality very great, has already been accomplished. At the present moment their decline has not only been arrested, but they are actually increasing in numbers, and improving in their social condition, (as at time of first publication). The proximate cause of this universal spectacle is to be found in their feeble attempts at agriculture; but the remote and the true one is to be discovered in the schools of the missionaries.

To these establishments among the Iroquois, from the days of the Jesuit fathers down to the present time, they are principally indebted for all the progress they have made, and for whatever prospect of ultimate reclamation their condition is beginning to inspire. By the missionaries they were taught our language, and many of the arts of husbandry, and of domestic life; from them they received the Bible and the precepts of Christianity. After the lapse of so many years, the fruits of their toil and devotion are becoming constantly more apparent: as, through years of slow and almost imperceptible progress, they have gradually emancipated themselves from much of the rudeness of Indian life. The Iroquois of the present day is, in his social condition, elevated far above the Iroquois of the seventeenth century. This fact is sufficient to prove that philanthropy and Christianity are not wasted upon the Indian; and further than this, that the Iroquois, if eventually reclaimed, must ascribe their preservation to the persevering and devoted efforts of those missionaries, who laboured for their welfare when they were injured and defrauded by the unscrupulous, neglected by the civil authorities, and oppressed by the multitude of misfortunes which accelerated their decline.

There are but two means of rescuing the Indian from his impending destiny; and these are education and Christianity. If he, will receive into his mind the light of knowledge, and the spirit of civilization, he will possess, not only the means of self-defence, but the power with which to emancipate himself from the thraldom in which he is held. The frequent attempts which have been made to educate the Indian, and the numerous failures in which these attempts have eventuated, have, to some extent, created a belief in the public mind, that his education and reclamation are both impossible. This enterprise may still, perhaps, be considered an experiment, and of uncertain issue; but experience has not yet shown that it is hopeless.

There is now, (as at time of first publication), in each Indian community in the state, a large and respectable class who have become habitual cultivators of the soil; many of whom have adopted our mode of life, have become members of the missionary churches, speak our language, are in every respect, discreet and sensible men. In this particular class there is a strong desire for the adoption of the customs of civilised life, and more especially for the education of their children, upon which subject often express the strongest solicitude. Among the youth who are brought up under such influences, there exists the same desire for knowledge, and the same readiness to improve educational advantages.

Out of this class Indian youth may be selected for a higher education, with every prospect of success, since to a better preparation for superior advantages, there is superadded a stronger security against a relapse into Indian life. In the attempted education of their young men, the prime difficulty has been to render their attainments permanent, and useful to themselves. To draw an untutored Indian from his forest home, and, when carefully educated, to dismiss him again to the wilderness, a solitary scholar, would be an idle experiment; because his attainments would not only be unappreciated by his former associates, but he would incur the hazard of being despised because of them. The education of the Indian youth should be general, and chiefly in schools at home.

A new order of things has recently become apparent among the Iroquois, which is favourable to a more general education at home, and to a higher cultivation in particular instances. The schools of the missionaries, established as they have been, and are, in the heart of our Indian communities, have reached the people directly, and laid the only true and solid foundation of their permanent improvement. They have created a new society in the midst of them, founded upon Christianity; thereby awakening new desires, creating new habits, and arousing new aspirations. In fact, they have gathered together the better elements of Indian society, and quickened them with the light of religion and of knowledge. A class has thus been gradually formed, which, if encouraged and strengthened, will eventually draw over to itself that portion of our Indian population which is susceptible of improvement and elevation, and willing to make the attempt, under the fostering care of the government, both state and national, and under the still more efficient tutelage of religious societies, great hopes may be justly entertained of the ultimate and permanent civilization of this portion of the Iroquois.

It is, indeed, a great undertaking to work off the Indian temper of mind, and infuse that of another race. It is necessary, to its accomplishment, to commence in infancy, and at the missionary school, where our language is substituted for the Indian language, our religion for the Indian mythology, and our amusements and mode of life for theirs. When this has been effected, and upon a mind thus prepared has been shed the light of a higher knowledge, there is not even then a firm assurance that the Indian nature is forever subdued, and submerged in that superior one which civilisation creates. In the depths of Indian society there is a spirit and a sentiment to which their minds are attuned by nature; and must be the power, and constant the influence, which can overcome the one, or eradicate the other.

In the education of the Iroquois, New York has recently made a commencement. Prior to 1846 our Indian youth were excluded from the benefits of the common school fund; their want of preparation for such schools furnishing, to some extent, a sufficient reason. At that time schools were first opened among them under appropriations from the public fund. These schools have not met with encouraging success; but their efficiency would have been much greater if they had been organized upon the boarding-school or missionary plan, instead of that of the common school. The former is the more practicable and successful system of Indian education; and it is greatly to be hoped that it will soon be adopted. To meet the growing demand for a higher education, the State Normal School, within the past year, (as at time of first publication), has not only been opened to a limited number of Indian youth, but a sufficient appropriation made for their maintenance while improving its advantages.

These two important events form an interesting era with the modern Iroquois. It remains only to give them permanent boarding-schools at home for the instruction of the mass of their youth, with access to the Normal School for their advanced scholars, and in a few years they will rise in the scale of intelligence, as far above their present level, as their fathers raised themselves, in the days of aboriginal sovereignty, above the level of cotemporary nations.

In addition to the special claim which the residue of the Iroquois have upon the people of the state, every principle of philanthropy pleads for the encouragement of their young men in their efforts to obtain a higher course of instruction than the limited earnings of Indian husbandry can afford. The time has come, in their social progress, when they are capable of a thorough intellectual training, and are able to achieve as high and accurate a scholarship as many of their white competitors. The time has also arrived when academical attainments will prove a blessing to themselves and to their families. By the diffusion of knowledge among them, the way will be facilitated for the introduction of the mechanic arts, and for their improvement in agricultural pursuits.

A small band of educated young men in each Indian community would find sufficient employment for their acquired capacities, in the various stations of teacher, physician, mechanic, and farmer; in each and all of which they would greatly promote the general welfare. If the desire for improvement, which now prevails among them, is met and encouraged, it will require but a few years to initiate them into the arts of civilised life, and to prepare them eventually for exercising those rights of property, and rights of citizenship, which are common to ourselves. How much more noble for the state to reclaim and save this interesting and peculiar portion of her people, than to accelerate their extinction by injustice; or to abandon them to their fate, when they are struggling to emancipate themselves by taking into their hands the implements of agriculture, and opening their minds to the light of knowledge.

There is no want of sympathy for their welfare among the people of New York; on the contrary, there is a widespread and deep-seated interest in their future reclamation. Whatever can be done to ameliorate their condition, and encourage that portion who have commenced the work of their own improvement, would receive the warmest commendation. If the Indian puts forth his hand for knowledge, he asks for the only blessing which we can give him in exchange for his birthright which is worthy of his acceptance.

The education and Christianization of the Iroquois is a subject of too much importance, in a civil aspect, to be left exclusively to the limited and fluctuating means of religious societies. The schools established and sustained among them by private benevolence, are, to the Indian, almost the same as common schools to our own people; and without them the Indian would, in times past, have been denied all means of instruction. These schools bring together the youth for elementary tuition, as a necessary preparation for moral and religious training. While there, they adopt, in all respects, the habits of civilised life, are taught our language, and the more simple elementary studies. In so far, it would be but a just act of public beneficence to allow those pupils to draw the same share of public money which falls to the other children of the slate.

A system of public Indian education, upon such a plan as their circumstances demand, should either be adopted by the state, or a portion of the public money bearing some proportion to the number of Indian pupils, should be placed at the disposal of the local missionary, to be expended with an equal portion contributed by private benevolence, or by the Indians themselves. It is time that our Indian youth were regarded, in all respects, as a part of the children of the state, and brought under such a system of tutelage as that relation would impose.

The vast extent of the religions enterprises of the present day has tended to draw the attention of the Christian world away from the Indian, into fields more distant, and perhaps more attractive. During the past sixty years, (as at time of first publication), the Iroquois have received but a small share of the Christian watchfulness to which their wants entitle them. Faithful and zealous missionaries, it is true, have laboured among them producing results far greater than is generally believed; but the inadequate scale upon which these missions were organized, and the fluctuations in their efficiency, which were inseparable from their irregular and limited supplies, have prevented them from carrying forward their work to its full completion. But whatever has been done, is chiefly to be ascribed to them, and to the denominations which they represent.

Too much cannot be said of the teachableness of the Indian, and of his aptitude to learn, when subjected to systematic discipline. If the same means, and the same influences which are employed to educate and elevate the mass of our own people, and without the constant application of which, they themselves would soon fall into ignorance, were brought to bear upon our Indian population, they would rise under it with a rapidity which would excite both surprise and admiration. Instances are not wanting among the present Iroquois, of attainments in scholarship which would do credit to any student. To give employment to those Indian youth whose acquired capacities would enable them to fill stations of trust and profit among ourselves, is another species of encouragement which commends itself to the generous mind. Both in our civil and social relations with the red men, we regard them as a distinct and separate class; when in each of these relations they should not only be regarded as our fellowmen, but as a part of our own people.

Born upon the soil, the descendants of its ancient proprietors, there is no principle which should make them aliens in the land of their nativity, or exclude them from any of those advantages which are reserved to ourselves. So far as they are able to appreciate and enjoy the same privileges which pertain to the mass of the people, the claim for participation which their situation silently puts forth should not be disregarded.

The lands of the Iroquois are still held in common, the title being vested in the people. Their progress toward a higher agricultural life has rendered this ancient tenure a source of inconvenience; although they are not as yet prepared for their division among the people. Each individual can improve and inclose any portion of their common domain, and sell or retain such improvements, in the same manner as with personal property; but they have no power to transfer the title to the land to each other, or to strangers. As early as the reign of James the Second, the right of purchasing Indian lands was made a government right exclusively, by royal proclamation; and it proved such a necessary shield against the rapacity of speculators, that this humane provision is still retained as a law in all the states of the Union, and by the national government.

When the Iroquois reach such a stable position, as agriculturists, as to make it safe to divide their lands among the several families of each nation, with the power of alienation, it will give to them that stimulus and ambition which separate rights of property are so well calculated to produce. The present system has at least the merit of saving all the people from poverty and vagrancy, if it does not enable a portion of them to become thrifty and substantial agriculturists. The first step towards the amelioration of their condition in this particular, would be a division among themselves, with the power of alienation to each other, under such restrictions as would be adapted to the case. This would serve to prepare the way for other changes, until finally they could be restored, with safety to themselves, not only to the full possession of those rights of property which are common to ourselves, but also to the rights and privileges of citizens of the state. When this time arrives, they will cease to be Indians, except in name.

The progressive elevation of our Indian population, here indicated, if carried to a successful result, would save but a portion of the Indian family; but that portion would become, in every respect, as useful and respectable as any other portion of our people. They would neither be wanting in ability, or morality, or public spirit; and perhaps it is not too much to conjecture, that specimens of the highest genius, and of the most conspicuous talent, hereafter destined to figure in the civil history of our republic, may spring from the ranks of the Indian citizens.

On the other hand, if they are left, unencouraged and unassisted, to struggle against their adverse destiny; or, more fatal still, if they are subjected to a false and unjust system of superintendence, the whole Indian family will ere long fade away, and finally become enshrouded in the same regretful sepulchre, in which the races of New England lie entombed.

The present system of national supervision is evidently temporary in its plan and purposes, and designed for the administration of our Indian affairs with the least possible inconvenience, rather than for their ultimate reclamation, to be followed by the bestowment of citizenship. It carries, upon all its features, the impression that the presence of the Indian upon this continent is temporary; and that he must inevitably surrender the remainder of his possessions, when he shall have become surrounded by the white man, and the summons be sent in for the customary capitulation. The sentiment which this system proclaims is not as emphatic as that emblazoned upon the Roman policy toward the Carthaginians—*Carthago est delenda*,—"Carthage must be destroyed;" but it reads in not less significant characters—*The destiny of the Indian is extermination.* This sentiment, which is so widespread as to have become a general theme for schoolboy declamation, is not only founded upon erroneous views, but it has been prejudicial to the Indian himself. If, then, public opinion and the national policy are both wrong upon these great questions, or if there are even strong grounds for suspecting them to be so, it becomes an act of justice, as well as of duty, to correct the one, and change the other.

Our Indian relations, from the foundation of the republic to the present moment, have been administered with reference to the ultimate advantage of the government itself; while the reclamation of the Indian has been a secondary object, if it ever entered into the calculation in the slightest degree. Millions of money, it is true, have been expended, and some show of justice preserved in their complicated affairs; but in all prominent negotiations the profit has been on the side of the government, and the loss on that of the Indian. In addition to this, instances of sharp-sighted diplomacy, of ungenerous coercion, and of grievous injustice, are to be found in the journal of our Indian transactions—a perpetual stigma upon the escutcheon of our republic. If references are demanded to the paragraphs, the reader may turn to that upon the Seminoles, or to the Georgia Cherokee treaty, executed by the government, or to the more recent treaties with the Iroquois themselves, in which the government bartered away its integrity, to minister to the rapacious demands of the Ogden Land Company.

Jefferson made the civilization of the Indian a subject of profound consideration, and a favourite element of the national policy during his administration. Washington at a still earlier period, regarded the future welfare of the Indian with deep solicitude. In founding the first system of intercourse and superintendence, he was guided by the most enlightened principles of justice and benevolence; and to such a degree were the Iroquois, in particular, impressed with the goodness and beneficence of his character, that they not only bestowed upon him, in common with other Indian nations, the appellation of *Father*, but to this day he is known among them as "The Great American." The aggressive spirit of the people, however, in connection with the slight estimation in which Indian rights were held, has ever been found too powerful an element to be stayed. It has had free course during the last sixty years, (as at time of first publication), until the whole territory east of the Mississippi, with inconsiderable exceptions, has been swept from the Indian. This fact renders any argument superfluous, to show, that within this period the reclamation and preservation of the red man has formed no part of the public policy.

But within the same period the moral elements of society have been developed and strengthened to such a degree as to work a change in public sentiment; kindlier feeling toward the Indian is everywhere apparent, joined with an unwillingness to allow him to be urged into further extremities. He has been sufficiently the victim of adverse fortune, to be entitled to a double portion of the interest and assistance of the philanthropist; and a new day, it is to be hoped, has already dawned upon his prospects.

It cannot be forgotten, that in after years our republic must render an account to the civilized world, for the disposal which it makes of the Indian. It is not sufficient, before this tribunal, to plead inevitable destiny; but it must be shown affirmatively, that no principles of justice were violated, no efforts were omitted, and no means were left untried, to rescue them from their perilous position. After all has been accomplished which the utmost efforts of philanthropy, and the fullest dictates of wisdom can suggest, there will still be sufficient to lament, in the unpropitious fate of the larger portion of the Indian family. It is the great office of the American people, first, to shield them against future aggression, and then to mature such a system of supervision and tutelage as will ultimately raise them from the rudeness of Indian life, and prepare them for the enjoyment of those rights and privileges which are common to ourselves.

To the Indian Department of the national government the wardship of the whole Indian family is, in a great measure, committed; thus placing it in a position of high responsibility. If any discrimination could be made between the several departments of the government, this should he guided by the most enlightened justice, the considerate philanthropy. Great is the trust reposed, for it involves the character of the white race, and the existence of the red. May it ever be quickened to duty by a vivid impression of its responsibilities, and never violate, for any consideration, the sacred trust committed to its charge.

# Appendix

## 1
### Tragedy of the Devil's Hole.
### By Ebenezer Mix, Esq.

The author and compiler of the first edition of this work took much pains to procure a correct statement of this transaction, as its details had never before been published. He procured the statement of Jesse Ware, then a resident at Fort Schlosser—an aged man, who, after the occurrence, had been for a long time an intimate friend and boon companion of William Stedman, the principal, if not the only person of the English party, who escaped this horrible massacre with life. This statement appears to have awakened inquiry, by which some errors have been detected, and some new information obtained; therefore. we give a remodelled statement of the affair, from all the materials now in our possession.

After Forts Niagara and Schlosser were taken from the French by the British, in July, 1759, Sir William Johnson, the British commander, made a contract with William Stedman to construct a portage road from Lewiston landing to Fort Schlosser, the distance of eight miles, to facilitate the transportation of provisions and military stores from one place to the other, and superintend the transportation of the same.

On the 20th of June, 1763, Mr. Stedman, in conformity to his agreement, having finished the road, started, for the first time, with twenty-five loaded wagons, from Lewiston to Fort Schlosser.

Sir William Johnson, being suspicious of the integrity of the Seneca Indians, although the French war was then ended, and amnesty between all parties, the Six Nations included, reciprocally declared, detached a party of fifty soldiers, with their officers, to escort Mr. Stedman's party. The Seneca Indians, who, from their late allies, the

French, had imbibed an inveterate hatred against the English, watched the progress of the construction of the road, and were determined to nip in the bud the first attempt to use it; as they considered it a trespass on their premises, and an infringement on their rights.

By means of their friendly intercourse with the English, they easily ascertained the time the first attempt would be made to cross the portage with teams. They accordingly congregated their whole force at that time, and lay in ambush on the Niagara River, about half-way between Lewiston and Fort Schlosser. At this place the road approaches within a few feet of the edge of the precipice, at an acute-angle in the eastern bank of the river, which descends from eighty to a hundred feet almost perpendicularly, into a hideous-looking dell, called the Devil's Hole.

As soon as the British transportation party arrived at this place, the Indians sallied from their ambuscade, inclosed the whole body of the English, and either killed on the spot, or drove off the banks, every soldier, officer, teamster, and assistant, amounting to near one hundred men, together with their horses, carriages, loading, and everything else pertaining to the expedition, except Mr. Stedman, the superintendent, who was on horseback.

A robust and gigantic Indian seized Mr. Stedman's horse by the bridle reins, and was leading him east to the woods, through the scene of deadly strife, probably for the purpose of devoting him to the, more excruciating torments of a sacrifice; but, while the captor's attention was drawn in another direction for a moment. Stedman, with his knife, cut the bridle reins near the bits, at the same time thrusting his spurs into the flanks of his well-trained charger, rode east into the forest—being the target of hundreds of Indian rifles, aimed at his person and flying steed, from which neither he nor his horse received the least injury. He continued his course east about two miles, where he struck Gill Creek, which he followed down to its mouth, and then down the bank of the Niagara River to Fort Schlosser.

From all the accounts of this barbarous transaction, Mr. Stedman was the only person belonging to his party who was not either driven or thrown off into the Devil's Hole. Tradition has transmitted to us various accounts of the fate of some few others of the party; that is, that one, two, or three others escaped with life, after being driven off the bank, although badly wounded and maimed by the fall. Most of the accounts agree in the escape of a little drummer, who was caught, while falling, in the limb of a tree, by his drumstrap, from which he extricated himself, and descended the body of the tree to the ground. The account of this escape is the most to be relied on, because the most probable. Pieces of the wreck of this expedition are to be found at the bottom of the Devil's Hole at the present day.

As no attempt was made by the Indians, in this affair, except in the case of Stedman, to take prisoners, scalp the dead, or procure plunder, it appears that those minor objects were entirely merged in the more exalted pursuit, (according to their views,) of destruction, blood, and carnage.

The escape of Mr. Stedman, not only from the iron grasp of one of their most athletic and powerful warriors, but from the shower of rifle balls discharged at him from the rifles of their best and most unerring marksmen, confounded the Indians with wonder and fear, furnishing a subject, whereon to feed their most absurd, superstitious whims. They at once pronounced him a favourite of the Great Spirit; and to appease its wrath, made Stedman a present of the tract of land he had encompassed in his retreat to Fort Schlosser; to wit, beginning at the Devil's Hole; thence running east, to Gill Creek; thence southerly, down the creek, to the Niagara River; thence down the river, to Niagara Falls; and thence northerly, still bounding on the river, to the place of beginning; being a tract about two miles wide, and three and a half miles long.

But neither the British government, nor the United Suites, or either of the states, has ratified or confirmed that gift; although Jesse Ware, claiming under Stedman, has, for a number of years in succession, assailed our legislative halls for the land, or some remuneration therefore. Nor does it appear that even the Indians themselves, after the excitement produced by the transaction had subsided, recognised any validity in Stedman's title; for the next year, 1764, they ceded the same tract, together with other lands, extending north to Lake Ontario, to the king of Great Britain, for a carrying-place around the Falls of Niagara.

2

GENERAL SULLIVAN'S EXPEDITION TO WESTERN NEW YORK.

During the years 1777 and 1778, the warriors of the Six Nations, the greater portion of the Oneidas excepted, bribed by British gold, clothing, rum, and gewgaws, and impelled by their natural thirst for blood—entirely disregarding all former treaties and pledges—attacked and laid waste the north-western frontier settlements of New York and Pennsylvania. Their footsteps were indelibly marked with the tomahawk and the scalping-knife, without regard to age, sex, or condition; and the destruction of all property on which the firebrand or rifle-ball could be made to take effect—as the valley of Wyoming, the fields of Cherry Valley,[1] and the banks of the Mohawk, bore melancholy testimony.

It became necessary for the safety, if not for the very existence of our border settlements, that these hired plunderers, incendiaries, and assassins should receive a signal chastisement for their predatory and barbarous incursions; not only as an act of retributive justice, but to deprive them of the means of repeating these atrocities. To effect this grand desideratum, in the spring of 1779 measures were taken to destroy their abodes and their means of subsistence—drive them from their retreats to more remote regions, and strike them with terror at the exterminating principles of the mode of warfare adopted; this being decided to be the only means of subduing, or crippling the strength of a faithless foe, whose treaties are made only to be broken, and who are seldom to be caught or found, except when, for motives of advantage, they choose to stay or to reveal themselves.

As no connected account of this transaction, in detail, has ever been published, to our knowledge, we are under the necessity of culling from all the sources now accessible, the most authentic materials to form a connected narrative. For these materials, we acknowledge ourselves indebted to Marshall's *Life of Washington*, the *British Annual Register*, the *Encyclopaedia Americana*, the *Researches of De Witt Clinton*, *Washington's Letters*, the statement of John Salmon, Esq., late of Groveland, Livingston County, N.Y., who was orderly sergeant in the rifle company commanded by Capt. Michael Simpson and Lieutenant Thomas Boyd, forming part of Sullivan's army; and last, although not least, the statements of our worthy friend Major Moses Van Campen, who bore a conspicuous part in the battle which took place on the Tioga, and now resides as a retired gentleman, in the valley of the Genesee.

The original plan of this important campaign was, that the country of the Six Nations should be entered by three divisions of the army

---

1. *Butler's Rangers* by Ernest Cruikshank, Henry U. Swinnerton & Isaac A. Chapman three accounts of the American War of Independence: *The Story of Butler's Rangers and the Settlement of Niagara* by Ernest Cruikshank, *The Story of Cherry Valley* by Henry U. Swinnerton & *Wyoming Valley a Sketch of Its Early Annals* by Isaac A. Chapman, also published by Leonaur.

at the same time. The principal body, composed of generals Maxwell, Hand, and Poor's brigades, together with a train of artillery, the whole consisting of about three thousand men, to rendezvous at Wyoming under the immediate command of Major General Sullivan; from whence to march up the Susquehanna, and enter the heart of the territory of the Six Nations, occupied by the Senecas and Cayugas. The second division, composed of General Clinton's command of about fifteen hundred, who had wintered at Schoharie, were to ascend the valley of the Mohawk, pass through the territories of the Oneidas, as they had adhered to the treaty of neutrality, and attack and lay waste the settlements of the Tuscaroras and Onondagas; after which they were to join General Sullivan in the Genesee country; and the third division, consisting of between five and six hundred men, under the command of Colonel Brodhead, to march from Pittsburgh up the Alleghany, and after laying waste the Seneca villages and settlements on that river, likewise to join General Sullivan, if necessary.

Before the troops destined for the grand expedition had been put in motion, owing to some unfortunate circumstances, an enterprise of less extent was projected by General Schuyler, and its execution carried into effect with complete success. On the nineteenth of April, Colonel Van Schaick, assisted by Lieutenant-Colonel Willet and Major Cochran, at the head of between five and six hundred men, marched from Fort Schuyler, (Utica,) and on the third day reached and surprised the Onondaga Indian settlements. In the first village which they attacked, they killed twelve Indians, and made thirty-four prisoners, including one white man; this giving the alarm, the Indians deserted the other villages, extending over a large territory, and fled to the woods.

The party then, without molestation, burned all their buildings, provisions, and other combustible property in the several villages killed their horses, cattle, and other stock, and utterly destroyed the whole settlement. With such precipitancy had the Indians fled from their villages, that they left about a hundred rifles and guns in their houses. The party having finished their work of destruction, returned to Fort Schuyler on the sixth day, without the loss of a man.

The eastern division of the army, under the command of General Clinton, marched to Schenectady in the month of May, and proceeded up the Mohawk in boats, overawing and putting to flight the remnant of the Mohawks, who were still hanging around their native valley. But in consequence of the principal object of their being assigned to that route, the destruction of the Onondaga settlements, having been accomplished by the enterprise of Colonel Van Schaick and his party, on their arrival at Canajoharie, General Clinton received orders from Major-General Sullivan, under whose command he was, to march his division to Otsego Lake, provide boats, and make other preparations to descend the eastern branch of the Susquehanna River, and meet him at Tioga Point when afterward directed.

Agreeable to orders, General Clinton marched his division to Otsego Lake, provided two hundred and eight boats, and necessary provision, threw a dam across the outlet, thereby raising the water in the lake two feet or over, to enable him, when he pleased, to cause a freshet in the river, to float his boats down with the greater rapidity and safety. He then waited for further orders. The main army, which rendezvoused at Wyoming, under the command of General Sullivan, for the want of supplies, and by reason of other adverse circumstances, did not leave that place until the last of July, when it marched to Tioga Point, where, on the 22nd of August, it was joined by the eastern division under General Clinton. After the junction of the two divisions, General Sullivan assumed the command in chief, having, for his immediate subordinates, Generals Clinton, Maxwell, Poor, and Hand, and Major Parr, of the rifle corps.

General Sullivan then marched up the Tioga River in search of the enemy, who, he had ascertained, were in some force, at no great distance on that route. On the 29th of August, at 11 o'clock, a.m., the enemy was discovered by the van-guard, about one mile below Newton, (now Elmira.) The whole force that the enemy were able to collect, amounting, according to Sullivan's account, to fifteen hundred, of whom two hundred were white Tories, known as Butler's Rangers, and the residue Indians, commanded by Brandt, the two Butlers, Grey, Guy Johnson, and McDonald, were here assembled, covered by a lengthy breastwork, rudely constructed of logs and felled trees, masked with pine and shrub-oak bushes stuck in the ground. The right flank of this work was covered by the river, and on their left, and in front, were two sharp ridges, parallel to each other, covered with parties of Indians, ready to fall on the right flank and rear of Sullivan's army, when it had progressed a sufficient distance within the ambuscade.

But the whole was discovered in sufficient time to guard against any disastrous results. General Poor was ordered to take possession of the outer ridge, turn the enemy's left flank, and attack him in the rear; while General Hand, aided by the artillery, attacked him in front.

General Poor, assisted by General Clinton, pushed his column up the hill, the van-guard of which was led by Major Van Campen, driving the Indians at the point of the bayonet—during which time a sharp conflict along the whole line of the breastwork was supported well on both sides. But the enemy, observing that their left flank was entirely exposed, and that they were in danger of being surrounded, as General Poor was proceeding with great rapidity, the savages, red and white, abandoned their breastwork, and, crossing the river, fled with the utmost precipitation.

This victory cost the Americans about thirty men. The ascertained loss of the Indians was also inconsiderable; but they were so intimidated, that they fled to, and deserted their villages, and abandoned the idea of farther resistance.

From Newtown, the army marched north, between the lakes, to the Seneca River; and detached parties were sent from their encampment in every direction, overrunning and laying waste the Indian settlements, cutting down their orchards, destroying their provisions and crops, killing their hogs, cattle, and horses—in short, applying the besom of destruction to everything that could afford shelter or sustenance to man or beast. If, indeed, the humane feelings of the Americans employed in this work of destruction sometimes prompted them to relent their own destructiveness, the watchword—Wyoming, Cherry Valley, or the Mohawk—would add a fresh impulse to the arm, and force the respiration of a fanning breeze to the faggot.

After finishing their labours in the east, the army proceeded west, for the purpose of closing its unopposed career of destruction at the chief village of the Senecas, Little Beard's Town, lying on the Genesee River. They passed the foot of Canandaigua Lake, meting out a full measure of destruction and desolation on the village and settlement at that place, as well as on the village at the outlet of the Honeoye. On their arrival at the head of Conesus Lake, within eight or nine miles of Little Beard's Town, they encamped on the ground, now known as Henderson's Flats.

Early in the evening, a party of twenty-one men was detached, and sent out under the command of Lieutenant Boyd, accompanied by a faithful Oneida Indian guide, for the purpose of reconnoitring in the vicinity of Little Beard's Town. Their first point of destination was an Indian village on the east side of Genesee River, nearly opposite the capital of the Senecas, to which it kind of suburb. On the arrival of the party at the village, they found that it had been lately deserted, as the fires in the huts were still burning. Being much fatigued, and the night being far spent, they encamped for the residue of the night in a secluded place near the village, sending two of their number back to the main army to report. In the morning they crept from their place of concealment, and discovered two Indians hovering about the settlement, one of whom was immediately shot and scalped by one of the riflemen, by the name of Murphy. Having thus exposed their presence in the place, Lieutenant Boyd, concluding that any further attempt to gain information would not only be useless, but rashly hazardous, ordered a retreat to the main army.

This little band retraced their steps until they arrived within a mile and a half of the camp, when they were intercepted by a party of observation from the enemy's camp. They fought desperately and rashly, for there was no chance to retreat. The result was, that twelve were killed, including their faithful guide. Lieutenant Boyd and a private by the name of Parker were taken prisoners, and the remaining seven made their escape by flight through the enemy's ranks, among whom was the brave but incautious Murphy. The dead of this little heroic band were left on the ground by the Indians, and Lieutenant Boyd and Parker were immediately conducted to Little Beard's Town.

When Lieutenant Boyd began to realize his situation as a prisoner of the Indians, he solicited an interview with Brandt, who, he knew, commanded his captors, and of whose character he had received some information. This chief immediately presented himself, when Lieutenant Boyd, by one of those appeals which are known only to those who have been initiated and duly instructed in certain mysteries, and which will never fail to bring succour to a "distressed brother," addressed him as the only source from which he could expect a respite from cruel punishment or a lingering and painful death. The appeal was recognised, and Brandt immediately, and in the strongest language, assured him that his life should be spared. Brandt, however, being called on to perform some particular service which required a few hours absence, left the prisoners in the charge of the British colonel, Butler, of the rangers.

As soon as Brandt had left, Butler commenced his interrogatories, to obtain from the prisoners a statement of the number, situation, and intentions of the army under General Sullivan, and threatened, in case they hesitated or prevaricated in their answers, to deliver them up to be massacred by the Indians, who, in Brandt's absence, and with the encouragement of their more savage commander, Butler, were ready to commit the greatest cruelties. Relying, probably, on the promises which Brandt had made them, and which undoubtedly he intended to fulfil, they refused to give Butler the desired information. Butler, upon this, hastened to put his threat into execution. They were delivered to some of their most ferocious enemies, who, after having put them to the most severe torture, killed them by severing their heads from their bodies.[2]

The main army, immediately after hearing of the disaster which befell Lieutenant Boyd's detachment, moved on toward Genesee River, and finding the bodies of those who fell in Boyd's heroic attempt to break through the enemy's ranks, buried them on the battle ground, which is now in the town of Groveland. Upon their arrival at the Genesee River, they crossed over and found Little Beard's Town and all the adjacent villages deserted. The bodies of Lieutenant Boyd and Parker were found and buried in one grave, near the bank of Little Beard's creek, under a clump of wild plum trees. Mr. Salmon was one who assisted in committing to the earth the remains of his friend and companion in arms, the gallant Boyd.

The army, having scoured the country for many miles up and down the river, burning all the Indian villages, and destroying all their corn, hogs, cattle, and other means of subsistence, finally, to close their labours of destruction, applied the torch to the ancient metropolis of the Seneca nation, Little Beard's Town, which contained one hundred and twenty-eight houses.

While General Sullivan had been fixing waste the Cayuga, and part of the Seneca settlement, the western division under Colonel Broadhead marched up the Alleghany River and French Creek. Here too, the Indians were totally unable to resist the force with which they were invaded. After one unsuccessful skirmish, they abandoned their villages and property, and fled to the woods for personal safety. Colonel Brodhead, having visited the settlements on French Creek, ascended the Alleghany to Olean Point, destroying all the Indian villages on French Creek and on the Alleghany River; and, ascertaining that it was not necessary for him to join the main army, he returned with his division to Pittsburgh, leaving Cattaraugus, Buffalo Creek, and Tonawanda settlements exempt from this general destruction.

General Sullivan, with the main army and the eastern division, having destroyed forty Indian villages, (including those destroyed by Colonel Van Schaick's party, and the western division under Colo-

2. See Mrs. Jemison's account, chapter 8.

nel Brodhead,) one hundred and sixty thousand bushels of corn, vast quantities of beans and other vegetables, a great number of horses, hogs, cattle, farming utensils, etc., and everything that was the result of labour or produce of cultivation—being the sanguinary achievement of three weeks unmolested and unremitting employment of between four and five thousand men—countermarched to Newtown. having been absent five weeks; thence past Tioga Point, Wyoming, and Easton, to New Jersey, where he went into winter quarters; having lost but about forty men during the whole campaign, either by sickness or the fortunes of war.

## 3.
### REMOVAL OF THE REMAINS OF BOYD.
### By Ebenezer Mix, Esq.

In the year 1841, some gentlemen in Rochester, and along the Genesee Valley, determined to pay a tribute of respect to the memory of Lieutenant Boyd and his companions, who fell or were sacrificed at Little Beard's Town and its vicinity, during General Sullivan's campaign, by removing their remains to Rochester, and reinterring them, with appropriate solemnities, in the new cemetery at Mount Hope.

The necessary preparations were made, by disinterring the remains, depositing them in the capacious urn, and raising a large mound of earth over the grave of Lieutenant Boyd, for a memorial. On the twentieth of August, 1841, a large concourse of people assembled at the village of Cuyler, among whom were several revolutionary patriots, and in particular Major Moses Van Campen, and two other fellow-soldiers who were with Boyd and his unfortunate companions, in Sullivan's army, when the urn containing the remains was removed from the top of the mound, under convoy of a military escort, composed of several independent companies, and a band of music from Rochester, to Colonel Cuyler's grove, near the village of Cuyler, where a pertinent and lucid, historical and biographical discourse was pronounced by ——Treat, Esq., after which, the remains were escorted to Rochester, by the military, music, citizens, etc., in several canal-boats. The next day, the remains were removed from the city of Rochester to Mount Hope, escorted as before, and attended by His Excellency, Governor Seward, his military suite, and an immense concourse of citizens. After an appropriate address by His Excellency, and an appeal to the throne of Grace by the Rev. Mr. E. Tucker, the remains were reinterred by the military with the honours of war.

# 4.

## THE GENESEE COUNTRY AS IT WAS AND IS.
## By Ebenezer Mix, Esq.

It may not be uninteresting to the reader, to compare the state of the "Genesee country" as it was eighty-two years ago, (as at time of first publication), when our narrative first introduced us into that region, with what it is now; and view the contrast.

Along the northern border of the district referred to, then too rude and desolate even for an Indian residence, the Erie Canal now winds its way, floating the products of the fertile regions of the west, to the great commercial emporium of the nation; and returning to the western agriculturists, contributions from the manufacturing establishments of every nation, and the productions of the soil of every clime.

The Genesee Valley Canal, now being constructed, is in a forward and progressive state, being now navigable from Rochester to Mount Morris. This canal extends from the Erie Canal at Rochester, up the west bank of Genesee River, and on the western margin of its flats, past Scottsville—near Fowlersville and Geneseo—through the village of Cuyler, and past Moscow, to Squawkie Hill and Mount Morris, having passed through the ancient sites of Cannewagus, Bigtree, Little Beard's and Squawkie Hill villages. At Squawkie Hill it crosses Genesee River *in a pond*, where it diverges from the river and pursues its course through the village of Mount Morris, and up to the valley of .the Canneskraugah Creek, to the Shaker settlement, in the town of Groveland; from which place a branch canal extends along the valley of the Canneskraugah to Dansville—the main canal here taking the valley of Cushaqua Creek, converging again toward the river, passing through the villages of Nunda Valley and Messenger's Hollow, reaches Genesee River again at Portageville, after having been carried through the "deep cut," necessary to disengage it from the valley of the Cushaqua; and the Tunnel upward of sixty rods in length, through the ridge of rock, mentioned in Chapter 5, as having, according to conjecture, once extended across the river, and filled its present channels above the upper falls.

At Portageville the canal is taken across the river in an aqueduct; it then traverses the western bank of the river, and the western margin of the flats, passing Mixville within half a mile of its centre, from which is constructing a navigable feeder into the canal; from thence it continues along the western margin of Canneadea Flats, to Black Creek, which approaches the river from the south The canal then passes up the valley of Black creek, to the summit level in the town of Cuba; thence across the summit level, about two miles through a marsh, to the waters of Oil Creek; thence down its valley, through the village of Cuba, to Hinsdale, at the junction of Oil and Ischua Creeks, whence the stream assumes the name of Olean Creek; thence down the Olean Valley to the village of Olean, on the Alleghany River, which is about fourteen miles above the Indian village of Unawaumgwa or Tuneunguan, introduced to our readers in the fourth and fifth chapters. It is a fact, however unimportant it may appear, that this canal, from Olean to Little Beard's Town, follows, with no material deviation, the old Indian path, or trail, which Mary Jemison travelled nearly a century ago, when she first came to Genishau.

Although the whole of the Genesee country is now checkered with groves, orchards, and fields; studded with villages, country seats, farmhouses, barns, and granaries; it will not be thought invidious to particularise the present situation of the localities especially referred to in the preceding pages.

The ground on which stood the great metropolis of the Senecas—Little Beard's Town—is now converted into fruitful corn and wheat fields; but adjoining is the village of Cuyler, which has sprung up, as it were by magic, since the Genesee Valley Canal became navigable to Mount Morris. The village of Geneseo, with its courthouse and other county buildings, churches, academies, and elegant private mansions, lies about three miles to the north-east, while Moscow, with its spacious public square, churches, academy, etc., lies two miles to the south-west. The sites of Bigtree and Cannewagus villages are known but as fertile fields, yielding abundant harvests; while on the east side of the Genesee, near Cannewagus, is the pleasant village of West Avon, and the Avon mineral springs, the medical properties of whose waters, and the romantic scenery displayed in its location and environs, render it, of late years, a desirable retreat for invalids and the infirm; and a fashionable resort for health and beauty. The old encamping ground at the "Big bend" is now occupied by the staid business village of Batavia, with its county buildings, five churches, female seminary, etc.

The Tonawanda, Tuscarora, Cattaraugus, and Buffalo Creek villages are still occupied by the remnant of the Senecas; but Tonawanda has its neighbouring villages of Akron and Caryville—Tuscarora its Lewiston, Cattaraugus its Lagrange, and the Buffalo Creek villages are closely bordered by the city of Buffalo, with its immense commerce, and all the various component parts, with the useful and ornamental appendages which constitute a city. Geneva occupies the ground on which General Sullivan captured a village containing one *papoose*; and the site of the "Old Castle" is now flanked by Castleton.

The Sabbatical and wealthy village of Canandaigua, with its elegant public and private edifices, stands in bold contrast with the midnight *powwows* of Cah-nan-dah-gwa, with its cluster of *wigwams*. Dansville takes its station "among the Slippery Elms," and improves, with commendable zeal, its manufacturing facilities. Although the site of the Squawkie Hill village is used for agricultural purposes only; in its vicinity, on the ground where stood one of Ebenezer or Indian Allen's *harems*, now stands the lively and pleasant village of Mount Morris. Above the Portage Falls is the village of Portageville, with its great water-power, and numerous factories. Near the site of the Lower Canneadea Indian village is the village of Mixville, with its church and other public buildings—its unrivalled facilities for using its permanent water-power and its present machinery propelled thereby. The Alleghany River villages are still occupied by the Indians, (as at time of first publication).

Near the month of Allen's Creek, between Mount Morris and Rochester, where stood Indian Allen's other *harem* the village of Scottsville. a flourishing business place; and at the northern succession of great falls on the Genesee, when Allen built the first apology for a grist-mill in the west, now stands the city of Rochester, with all its superb public and private edifices, its commerce, and manufactures, together with its hundred run of stones in its flouring-mills, manufacturing more flour annually than is produced at any other place on the globe.

Some idea of the improvements in a social and religious point of view which have taken place on this territory within less than thirty years may be drawn from the following fact:

In the year 1811, there was standing near the Caledonia Springs a wood-coloured house, without porch, steeple, dome, or tower, to denote its use. This building was occupied as a Scotch Presbyterian meeting-house; and it was at that time the only building erected or exclusively used for Divine Worship in the State of New York, on or west of Genesee River, although the territory then contained at least twenty-five thousand inhabitants.

During the three following' years, this territory was the scene of

165

a border warfare, in which no age or sex was exempt from slaughter, and no edifice too sacred for the application of the torch. The observance of the Sabbath was merged in the tumults of the camp; and the din of battle, with its martial music, usurped the place of the deep-toned organ and the harmonious choir; while the full voice of the commanding chief silenced the persuasive eloquence of the apostolic minister—the messenger of peace.

This territory now contains two large cities, and is thickly interspersed with thriving villages;—the cities contain numerous houses for public worship; each village is provided with from one to five; and in the back farming towns, where there is no compact settlement deserving the name of a village, the eye of the traveller will scarcely lose sight of one or more of those spires, cupolas, or towers, pointing toward the skies, emphatically proclaiming to his mental ear, as from the surrounding habitations, "*We, Too, Worship God.*"